~~HIKING TRAILS~~
OF CENTRAL COLORADO

Cover photos by Gordon McKeague/Bill Bueler
All other photos by the author except as noted.

HIKING TRAILS
OF CENTRAL COLORADO

Bob Martin

Third Edition

PRUETT **P** PUBLISHING COMPANY
Boulder, Colorado

Third Edition

3   4   5   6   7   8   9

Printed in the United States of America

Library of Congress Cataloging in Publication Data

Martin, Bob, 1920-
   Hiking trails of central Colorado.

   Includes index.
   1. Hiking—Colorado—Guide-books.
2. Trails—Colorado—Guide-books. 3 Colorado—
Description and travel—1981-   —Guide-books. I. Title.
GV199.42.C6M37 1983   917.88   82-25067
ISBN 0-87108-787-1 (pbk.)

Contents

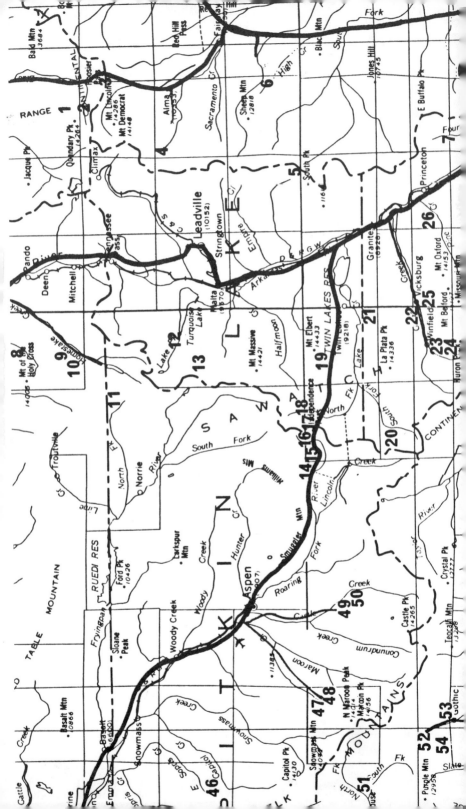

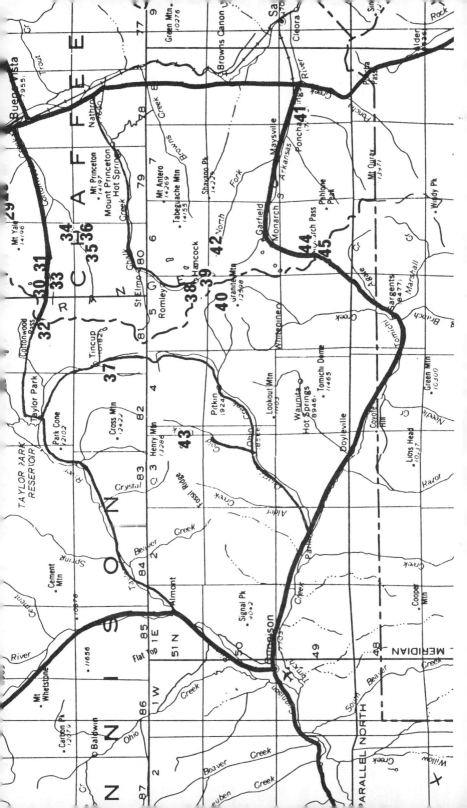

Introduction

The mountains of central Colorado are truly the high points of the state. The Sawatch Range forms the spine of the Continental Divide for nearly a hundred miles. The divide also passes through the Mosquito Range to the east. The more rugged and scenic Elk Mountains are west of the Sawatch. These mountain ranges are the territory for the hikes and climbs described in this book.

These three mountain ranges include almost half of the high mountain peaks of Colorado—they have twenty-six of the fifty-four Colorado summits over 14,000 feet, including the three highest. There are twenty-three other peaks in this area that rank in the highest hundred in the state.

High mountains alone don't necessarily make for enjoyable hiking and climbing. However, there are many other reasons why this area is prime hiking country. Prolific mining activity many years ago has not only left interesting buildings and equipment to visit, but also has created a network of roads and trails, making it easier to reach the high country. Much of the country is within one of six national forests, and a good portion is situated in several wilderness areas. Most of the wooded areas are relatively open, making bushwhacking not as difficult as it is in many areas. Most of the slopes and ridges in the Sawatch and Mosquitos provide enjoyable walking. Finally, the weather is not as severe as it is in some other mountain areas of the state.

The Mosquito Range has high but quite rounded ridges and summits, and much of the high country climbing is easy walking. It has a wealth of interesting mining relics. Its network of roads provides easy access to most of the high country.

The Sawatch Range is more varied. Its greater length and width permit some large areas that require long day hikes or backpacks

1

to reach some objectives. While many of the high mountain climbs are relatively dull, long grinds, a variety of scenic hikes can lead you to numerous interesting destinations. The terrain makes for attractive off-trail hiking of easy or moderate difficulty.

The Elk Range is more rugged and scenic. A main hiking area in the Elks is the Maroon Bells-Snowmass Wilderness with its network of excellent trails. The high peaks of the Elk Range are more difficult to climb, and some require technical skills.

How can we choose only fifty-five hikes in such an area? There are literally hundreds from which to select. My wife, Dotty, and I have been hiking in this area for about fifteen years. We've taken several hundred day hikes from our home near Buena Vista, rarely to the same place. Yet, we still have dozens of hikes on our "to do" list.

First, the hikes described in this book are ones that can be completed in a day. True, most any of them could be extended into an overnight backpack, if that's what you like. The hikes selected cover a range of territory, with trailheads accessible from many different localities. Most hikers like a specific objective for a hike destination. The hikes in this book visit a variety of mountains, passes, and lakes. The level of difficulty ranges from quite easy to somewhat difficult. The time required varies from a few hours to a long day.

In selecting the hikes to be included, those that make a good loop trip are favored, giving more different scenery per mile of hiking. Preference is also given to hikes that will be enjoyable even if the objective isn't reached. On the loop trips, if you haven't gotten halfway around the loop, you can always return the way you came.

Many beginning hikers prefer to stick to hikes on trails, but as they gain experience, they become more interested in off-trail hiking. So these hikes include many that are off the trail. None require technical climbing skills or equipment. For some of the hikes, the route chosen is not the easiest or the quickest to reach the objective. I've favored a route that is most interesting, varied, and scenic.

The hikes in this book can be completed by persons in good physical condition, whether or not they have had a lot of hiking experience. However, those without hiking experience and those not acclimated to the high, central Colorado altitudes initially should stick to the easier trail hikes.

The hikes will take you to a number of high peaks, including several over 14,000 feet and several more in the state's highest hundred. There are a number of lower summits that are even more interesting. You'll walk lots of trails, climb steep slopes, bushwhack through the forest, walk through valleys, visit high lakes, view numerous relics of old mines, walk interesting ridges, and, in general, get lots of exercise.

But What if I Just Want to Climb the Fourteeners?

You've got the wrong book. The only Fourteeners included here are several climbs via routes different than the "traditional" ones. These routes may be longer or more difficult but are ones that we've found to be more interesting. Many climbers visit the Sawatch or Mosquitos just to climb the Fourteeners and therefore miss some of the best hiking in the area. We think that you'll enjoy these hikes more. Several of the Fourteeners in the Elks are fine climbs but are more difficult than those included in this book.

A number of guides are available for climbing all of the Colorado Fourteeners. The most complete is *A Climbing Guide to Colorado's Fourteeners* by Borneman and Lampert (Pruett Publishing Company). The classic *Guide to the Colorado Mountins* by Bob Ormes gives brief climbing descriptions on all the Fourteeners as well as many other mountains. The Colorado Mountain Club publishes a *Condensed Climbing Guide to the Fourteeners*. Don't ask what it's condensed from.

Choosing the Right Hike

At the beginning of each hike description, tabular information is listed to give a brief overview of the hike. **Distance** is the total length of the hike in miles. It is the round-trip distance in the case of out and back hikes. Such distances can only be approximate, since trail and cross-country measurements cannot be made with great accuracy.

Following the distance, in parentheses, is an indication of the type of hike the distance covers. An **out and back** hike returns on the same route that it covered in reaching the destination. A **loop** hike returns to the trailhead by an entirely different route, not retracing the route at all. A **keyhole loop** has an out and back section at one end and a loop at the other. A **dumbbell loop** has an out and back section at each end with a loop in the middle. A **point-to-point** hike begins at one place and ends at another, without retracing the route.

Starting elevation, in feet, is the elevation at the trailhead. **High point** reached on the hike is shown in feet. **Elevation gain** is at least as great as the difference between the high point and starting elevation and is often greater if there are losses of elevation that must be regained.

Rating is a subjective judgment of the difficulty of the hike. **Easy** hikes are generally all on a trail or on easily walked cross-country routes. **Moderate** hikes usually involve some steep slopes, boulder hopping, or bushwhacking, or may be long hikes on easier terrain. **Difficult** hikes usually involve rock scrambling using the hands, more difficult bushwhacking, very steep slopes, or route finding problems, or may be extremely long. These ratings are only intended to divide the hikes into groups. Many experienced mountaineers would find all of these hikes easy, while some newcomers to mountain hiking will find some of the easy ones to be difficult.

Time allowed is an estimate of the time it will take the average party to complete the hike. It allows time for brief rests and a quick lunch but represents, mainly, continuous walking.

On many of these hikes you may be able to return from the objective in a shorter time than it took you to get there. But don't depend on it. Often the combination of difficult terrain, tiredness, moving slower after eating, or deteriorating weather can make the return as time-consuming as the ascent. Therefore, it's best to start back when you've used up half the time you've allotted for the hike. In addition, the allotted time should provide a safety factor to bring you back to the trailhead before dark.

The **Maps** refer to U.S. Geological Survey topographic maps and the national forest maps on which the area of the hike is shown. Topographic maps, beyond the reduced portion shown in this book, are more essential for the difficult and off-trail hikes. The USGS 7.5 minute maps are available for all areas in which there are hikes in this book, and these 7.5 minute maps are listed in the tabular data. USGS county maps, which show topography in a smaller scale, cover a wider territory than the 7.5 minute maps and may be helpful. Names and elevations in the text are from the latest maps. The national forest maps are most useful for general orientation, getting to the trailhead, and picking out distant landmarks from the high points.

Just Follow the Trail Sign. What Sign?

That's one of the unfortunate aspects of present-day hiking. Many trail guides have been written on the assumption that the trail signs that the author saw would still be there when the readers took the same hike. Sad to report, that's not the case. Vandalism of trail signs is ever increasing. Often, you'll see a post where the sign once stood. Sometimes you'll see just a portion of a sign. In some cases, signs have been moved to the wrong location, perhaps deliberately. The forest service has made a valiant effort to combat this growing vandalism by installing more durable, if less picturesque, trail markers, such as those of heavy metal welded to large posts set in concrete.

Therefore, this guide is written without reference to trail signs. You'll see some, but when you do, consider it a bonus. Occasionally in the remote areas, there are some quaint old signs, but near the roads such signs have mostly disappeared. Don't worry about differing mileages on signs. They represent differing measurement techniques of different eras. When we last walked one of the hikes in this book, there was a sign giving the mileage to the destination. After a half mile we came to a second sign asserting that the destination was a mile further away than the distance shown on the first sign.

What's the Best Hike for Tomorrow?

Suppose you've picked out one or two dozen hikes that you're most interested in taking. What's the best one to take now? Selecting a hike appropriate for the conditions may be more important than picking the hike you like the most.

These hikes are intended for the summer hiking season, which may extend from May or June to October or November. In the early season, hikes on the southern slopes that don't go to high levels in the forest and that stay out of deep valleys are likely to be best. If the mornings are cold, pick hikes that will put you on eastern or southern slopes early in the day. During the hottest weather, you may prefer hikes on the northern slopes that provide a good percentage of shaded forest travel.

If it's likely to be windy, avoid those hikes with a lot of above timberline ridge walking. If the wind is from the north, favor a hike on the southern slopes. Hikes with a lot of high ridge travel are best in the late season after most of the snows are gone. Avoid the long ridge walks in the thunderstorm seasons. Such hikes can get you isolated a long way from your vehicle, with no good escape routes.

The table "Hike Destinations" (which follows this Introduction) lists the objectives of the hikes included in this book. Use the table to pick out any particular mountains, passes, or lakes that you'd like to visit. The table includes some of the alternate destinations that may be easily reached but that are not the primary objective of a given hike.

The table "Trailhead Data" (which follows "Hike Destinations") gives information that can help in selecting hikes. This table, plus the map of the general area, can help locate the hikes most convenient for you. This table shows the elevation of each trailhead. It shows the distance to the nearest designated forest service campground, if there is one closer than the nearest town. Forest service campgrounds are sometimes closed, either seasonally or at other times. The location of alternate campgrounds is usually posted at closed campgrounds. Most towns have nearby commercial campgrounds. There are usually good camping spots near the trailheads. The distance to the nearest town (large enough to have motels, food, and supplies) is also shown.

The next column shows the amount of unpaved road that must be driven to reach the trailhead. The last column indicates the amount that the hike can be shortened, if any, by use of a four-wheel drive (4WD) vehicle.

For information on equipment, getting in good physical condition, weather, finding your way, climbing techniques, first aid, and such subjects, refer to the many good books on these topics. Good hiking!

I'll take the responsibility of trying to describe these hikes to the best of my ability at the time I took them, updated with any information that has come to my attention since then. You'll have to take the responsibility for using good judgment when going on the hikes. Choose a hike within your ability, turn back in bad weather, allow plenty of time, and have the proper equipment.

My wife, Dotty, has gone on almost all of these hikes with me. She has also edited and typed the manuscript and has made countless suggestions for improvement. She has also been invaluable in helping to select the hikes to be included in this book from the hundreds that we have taken together in this area.

Others who have gone on one or more of these hikes with us include Dick Altman, Bill Davis, Ed and Jean Johnson, Charley McCall, Bobby and Gordon McKeague, Jerry and Jean Scott, and Art Tauchen. We enjoyed their companionship and appreciate the help that some of them and others have given in compiling information.

HIKE DESTINATIONS

Elevation, Feet	Destination	Hike No.
	Mountains	
14,197	Mount Belford	25
14,196	Mount Yale	29
14,153	Mount Oxford	26
14,073	Mount Columbia	28
14,003	Huron Peak	24
13,951	Fletcher Mountain	2
13,950	Pacific Peak	1
13,933	Mount Hope	22
13,908	Casco Peak	19
13,841	Hagerman Peak	51
13,841	unnamed (near Pacific Peak)	1
13,781	Mosquito Peak	4
13,761	Deer Mountain	18
13,739	Ptarmigan Peak	5
13,711	Twining Peak	17
13,635	Electric Pass Peak	49
13,626	unnamed (on Mount Princeton massif)	36
13,614	North Star Mountain	3
13,572	Weston Peak	5
13,523	Browns Peak	24
13,500	unnamed (near Independence Pass)	17
13,462	Treasury Mountain	54
13,380	East Geissler Mountain	16
13,326	West Buffalo Peak	7
13,301	West Geissler Mountain	16
13,300	East Buffalo Peak	7
13,300	Mount Daly	46
13,292	Waverly Mountain	26
13,271	Whitney Peak	9
13,248	unnamed (near Notch Mountain)	8
13,233	Turner Peak	30
13,203	unnamed, Williams Mountains	15
13,139	Savage Peak	11
13,132	Sewanee Peak	42

HIKE DESTINATIONS

Elevation, Feet	Destination	Hike No.
13,095	Mount Kreutzer	32
13,078	unnamed (near Green Timber Gulch)	35
13,055	unnamed (near Mount Kreutzer)	32
13,033	unnamed, Williams Mountains	14
12,893	Galena Mountain	12
12,818	Sheep Mountain (Mosquito Range)	6
12,792	unnamed (near Mount Kreutzer)	32
12,580	unnamed (near Mount Kreutzer)	32
12,486	Brittle Silver Mountain	40
12,442	Mount Poor	38
12,380	Central Mountain	40
11,939	Sheep Mountain, south summit (Sawatch)	34
11,858	Sheep Mountain, north summit (Sawatch)	34
11,844	unnamed (on Monarch Ridge)	44
	Passes	
13,500	Electric Pass	49
13,220	Elkhead Pass	25
13,186	Mosquito Pass	4
12,900	Triangle Pass	53
12,860	Red Mountain Pass	20
12,820	Lost Man Pass	16
12,705	Pearl Pass	50
12,580	Copper Pass	53
12,580	Willow Pass	47
12,580	Fall Creek Pass	9
12,500	West Maroon Pass	48
12,462	Buckskin Pass	47
12,380	Frigid Air Pass	52
12,380	Fancy Pass	10
12,167	Gunsight Pass	43
12,140	Chalk Creek Pass	39
12,100	Hasley Pass	52
12,020	Browns Pass (Sawatch Range)	31
12,020	Napoleon Pass	37

HIKE DESTINATIONS

Elevation, Feet	Destination	Hike No.
11,986	Missouri Pass	10
11,980	Tomichi Pass	40
11,940	Altman Pass	38
11,841	Midway Pass	14
11,840	South Fork Pass	15
11,766	Williams Pass	38
11,740	Oh-be-joyful Pass	55
11,700	Yule Pass	54
11,420	Buffalo Pass	7
11,372	Browns Pass (Mosquito Range)	6
10,860	Marshall Pass	45
	Lakes	
12,490	Independence Lake	16
12,132	Ptarmigan Lake	33
12,000	Seven Sisters Lakes	9
11,805	Lake Ann	23
11,760	Willis Lake	21
11,700	Lamphier Lake	43
11,675	Treasure Vault Lake	10
11,660	Hancock Lake	39
11,600	Capitol Lake	46
11,540	Fancy Lake	10
11,500	Missouri Lakes	10
11,340	Pass Creek Lake	41
11,300	Hunky Dory Lake	9
11,044	Savage Lake	11
10,936	Geneva Lake	51
10,560	Lost Man Reservoir	15
10,280	Harvard Lakes	27
	Other	
11,600	Old Alpine Tunnel	38
11,560	Hagerman Tunnel	13

Hike No.	Trailhead	Elevation, Feet
1	McCullough Gulch	11,035
2	Blue Lakes Reservoir	11,700
3	Hoosier Pass	11,539
4	Mosquito Pass road	11,520
5	Weston Pass	11,921
6	Browns Pass road	10,000
7	Fourmile Creek road	9,220
8	Half Moon Campground	10,300
9	off Homestake Reservoir road	10,280
10	off Homestake Reservoir road	10,020
11	off Fryingpan River road	9,880
12	west of Turquoise Lake	9,960
13	Hagerman Pass road	10,940
14	Independence Pass road	10,500
15	Independence Pass road	10,500
16	Independence Pass road	11,506
17	Independence Pass	12,093
18	Independence Pass road	10,794
19	Independence Pass road	9,970
20	South Fork Lake Creek road	10,940
21	Independence Pass road	9,280
22	Clear Creek road	9,850
23	south of Winfield	10,250
24	south of Winfield	10,250
25	Vicksburg	9,660
26	Pine Creek road	8,920
27	North Cottonwood Creek road	9,420

Nearest Campground, Miles	Nearest Town, Miles	Miles Un-Paved	Miles Less by 4WD
—	Breckenridge—9½	2	none
—	Breckenridge—9½	2	none
—	Breckenridge—10	none	3
—	Fairplay—12	7	3
Veston Pass—4½	Leadville—18	11	none
—	Fairplay—6½	3	5
—	Buena Vista—9	7½	3
alf Moon—0	Minturn—10	8	none
old Park—5	Minturn—21½	11½	3
old Park—3	Minturn—19½	9½	none
k Wallow—4	Basalt—34	7	none
lay Queen—1	Leadville—10	none	none
lay Queen—7½	Leadville—12½	4½	none
ost Man—0	Aspen—14	none	none
ost Man—½	Aspen—14½	none	none
ost Man—4	Aspen—18	none	none
ost Man—6	Aspen—20	none	none
win Peaks—10	Aspen—25	none	1
win Peaks—2½	Leadville—27½	none	none
win Peaks—9	Leadville—34; Aspen—34	4½	5
arry Peak—½	Leadville—23½	none	none
—	Buena Vista—24½	9½	none
—	Buena Vista—27	12	4
—	Buena Vista—27	12	4
—	Buena Vista—23	8	none
—	Buena Vista—13½	½	4
—	Buena Vista—6¾	4½	none

11

Hike No.	Trailhead	Elevation, Feet
28	North Cottonwood Creek road	9,420
29	North Cottonwood Creek road	9,420
30	Cottonwood Pass road	11,160
31	Cottonwood Pass road	9,900
32	Cottonwood Pass	12,126
33	Cottonwood Pass road	10,675
34	west of Cottonwood Lake	9,620
35	west of Cottonwood Lake	10,270
36	west of Cottonwood Lake	9,600
37	near Tincup	10,200
38	Hancock	11,040
39	Hancock	11,040
40	Tunnel Gulch road	11,100
41	Pass Creek road	9,220
42	near North Fork Reservoir Campground	11,480
43	Gold Creek Campground	10,030
44	Monarch Pass	11,300
45	Monarch Pass	11,300
46	Capitol Creek road	9,400
47	Maroon Lake parking area	9,580
48	Maroon Lake parking area	9,580
49	Ashcroft road	9,880
50	Ashcroft road	9,780
51	near Crystal	9,000
52	Schofield Park	10,400
53	near Gothic	9,820
54	Paradise Divide	11,260
55	Slate River road	8,940

ATA

Nearest Campground, Miles	Nearest Town, Miles	Miles Un-Paved	Miles Less by 4WD
—	Buena Vista—6¾	4½	none
—	Buena Vista—7	4¾	none
ollegiate Peaks—5½	Buena Vista—17	10	none
ollegiate Peaks—½	Buena Vista—12	5	none
ollegiate Peaks—8½	Buena Vista—20	13	none
ollegiate Peaks—3½	Buena Vista—15	8	none
ottonwood Lake—¼	Buena Vista—11¼	4¼	1
ottonwood Lake—3	Buena Vista—14	7	none
ottonwood Lake—¼	Buena Vista—11¼	4¼	none
irror Lake—3	Gunnison—40	10	1
ascade—11	Buena Vista—28	12	½
ascade—11	Buena Vista—28	12	3½
uartz—8½	Gunnison—35	10	3
—	Salida—12	4½	3
orth Fork—½	Salida—19	8	2
old Creek—0	Gunnison—29	7	none
onarch Park—3	Salida—23	none	none
onarch Park—3	Salida—23	10	none
—	Aspen—23½	7½	none
aroon Lake—¼	Aspen—10	none	none
aroon Lake—¼	Aspen—10	none	none
—	Aspen—13	½	none
—	Aspen—14	1	11
ogan Flats—11	Carbondale—34	5½	3
othic—5	Crested Butte—15	11	2
very Peak—1½	Crested Butte—9	5	none
othic—6½	Crested Butte—16½	12½	1
—	Crested Butte—5½	4½	10

13

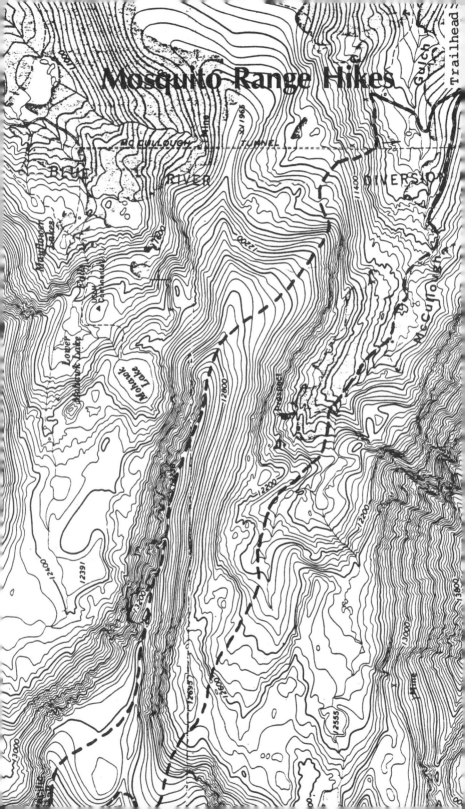

Mosquito Range Hikes

1. PACIFIC PEAK

Distance: 8 miles (loop)
Starting elevation: 11,035 feet
High point: 13,950 feet
Elevation gain: 3,300 feet
Rating: difficult
Time allowed: 8 to 10 hours
Maps: 7.5 minute Breckenridge
    Arapaho National Forest

Five of the Colorado peaks over 14,000 feet are in the Mosquito Range. The Mosquitos have eight other peaks over 13,800 feet that rank in the state's highest hundred. In general, these latter summits are the more interesting Mosquito Range climbs. Pacific Peak is one of the best.

Drive on Colorado 9 seven and a half miles south of Breckenridge or fourteen miles north of Fairplay. Two miles north of Hoosier Pass, the road makes a big curve to the west. Just north of the western part of this curve, take the good gravel road west. Take the north (right) fork at 0.15 mile, just after the road bends west. Follow this road for 1.6 miles to a fork at 11,035 feet. Park here.

Walk up the right fork, which descends 200 feet to cross McCullough Gulch and then climbs to a mine property at 11,100 feet. Climb up the hillside to the north, and then bear generally northwest to reach the east ridge of Pacific Peak at about 12,500 feet. Follow the ridge westward, first on an easy stretch, and then over some slow, rocky sections. Enjoy the view of Quandary Peak to the south, and notice Pacific Peak looming up as a distinctly pointed summit slightly north of west along the ridge.

After negotiating the ridge for a mile and a half, you'll come to a high flat area at 13,400 feet, one of the largest such areas in the high country. A large lake sits to the west in this area. Pass to the right of the lake and continue up the slope—an elevation gain of 550 feet—to reach the summit.

The suggested descent follows a different route. Come down the ridge to the south and continue to a saddle at 13,380 feet, between Pacific and the peak to the south. For an addition to the hike, you may want to climb this unnamed 13,841-foot peak to the

Pacific Peak as seen from Crystal Peak. The long ridge ascending from left to right is the climbing route. (photo by Gordon McKeague)

south. It's an easy 461 feet of elevation gain to the summit, which brings you to another of Colorado's highest 100 peaks. The reasons for such an additional climb would be "because it's there" or "I'll never be any closer," and not because of any particular distinction of that summit. If you do climb it, return toward Pacific Peak to the saddle.

From the 13,380-foot saddle, the return route descends to the east down McCullough Gulch. Start out by heading for the small lake at 12,695 feet. This is the steepest part of the return, and care must be exercised on the rocky slope.

Continue on down through the basin toward the left side of a long, narrow lake at 11,900 feet. Stay left of the outlet from this lake, and soon you should find a trail leading through a wooded area. This trail crosses to the south side of McCullough Gulch and leads to a road that will return you to the junction where the hike began.

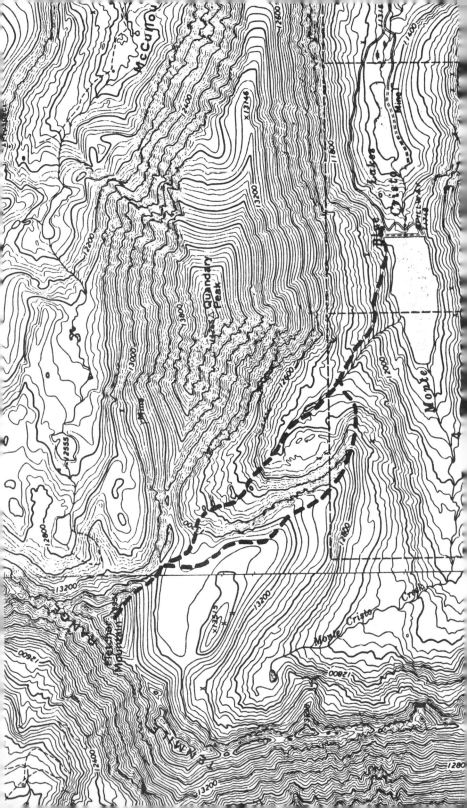

2. FLETCHER MOUNTAIN

Distance: 6 miles (dumbbell loop)
Starting elevation: 11,700 feet
High point: 13,951 feet
Elevation gain: 2,400 feet
Rating: moderate
Time allowed: 7 hours
Maps: 7.5 minute Breckenridge
      7.5 minute Copper Mountain
      Arapaho National Forest

Fletcher Mountain is an interesting and satisfying climb, much more so than climbs of the slightly higher Fourteeners in the area. It brings you into some of the most scenic and rugged parts of the Mosquito Range, although the hike itself is not difficult.

Drive on Colorado 9 seven and a half miles south of Breckenridge or fourteen miles north of Fairplay. Two miles north of Hoosier Pass, the road makes a big curve to the west. Go west on Summit County 850. Take the left fork at 0.15 mile, and continue two more miles to park just below the north end of the dam at Blue Lakes Reservoir.

Climb up the steep slope to reach the north end of the dam. Get on a trail along the north side of the reservoir. After about a hundred yards on this trail, climb steeply up the gravel slopes to the right to reach another trail that skirts the reservoir high on the slopes to the north.

Continue on this excellent trail until it reaches some mine buildings on the east side of the north inlet to the reservoir. Cross the creek to the west and head for the nose of the ridge directly west. Climb to the crest of this ridge on grassy benches and rocky slopes. Continue west and then northwest on the crest of this ridge to reach a very large flat area at about 13,350 feet. Descend a bit, and cross this flat area northward to reach the southeast ridge of Fletcher Mountain. From here, it's a climb of 600 feet up the rocky ridge to the summit. The best footing is along the crest of the ridge.

For most of the route you get a fine view of the vast Monte Cristo Creek basin and the jagged ridge running south from Fletcher Mountain to Wheeler Mountain. From the top there's a good view to

Pacific Peak from Fletcher Mountain. (photo by Bill Bueler)

the west of the large tailings ponds of the molybdenum operation in the Fremont Pass area. To the southwest is a view of what was once 13,555-foot Bartlett Mountain, which has been lowered by mine digging. To the east is Quandary Peak, its ruggedness on this side in sharp contrast to the easy route to the top from the east.

The imposing ridge point a half mile southwest looks almost as high as Fletcher. Don't be tempted to follow the jagged ridge from there south to Wheeler Mountain. Just return to the large flat area.

An alternate return from the flat area takes you east and then southeast into the basin between the ascent route and Quandary Peak. Follow the watercourse down this basin to reach the mine buildings and the trail back to the reservoir. This alternate return route is only for those looking for something a little harder to do. Others may elect to go back down the ridge route.

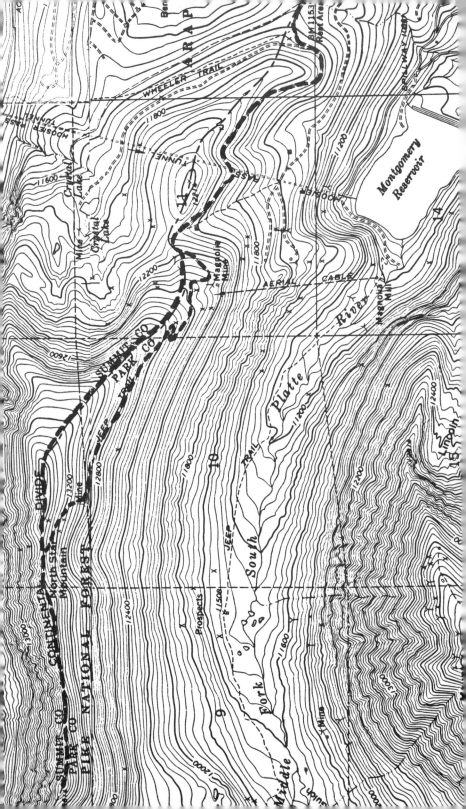

3. NORTH STAR MOUNTAIN

Distance: 8 miles (dumbbell loop)
Starting elevation: 11,539 feet
High point: 13,614 feet
Elevation gain: 2,400 feet
Rating: moderate
Time allowed: 7 hours
Maps: 7.5 minute Alma
7.5 minute Breckenridge
Arapaho National Forest
Pike National Forest

This hike takes you to a high mountain in the Mosquito Range surrounded by 14,000-foot peaks and other high summits. However, it's a mountain much less frequently climbed than the Fourteeners or even the higher Thirteeners in the area. Thus, you probably can have the mountain all to yourself and not be bothered by streams of climbers as on the higher peaks.

The starting point is at Hoosier Pass, on Colorado 9, twelve miles north of Fairplay and ten miles south of Breckenridge. There's a parking area on the west side of the highway. It would be possible to shorten the hike by about three miles with a 4WD vehicle, or sometimes even with a regular car, but for a hike of this distance, it's more interesting to start hiking from the pass.

Hike along the 4WD road to the west, bearing left to contour around a small hill. In the valley below to the south is Montgomery Reservoir, and across the valley is the vast Lincoln Amphitheater, on the east flank of Mount Lincoln. After about a mile and a half, you'll reach a saddle at 12,100 feet. Continue a couple of hundred yards along the 4WD road as it starts to contour left around the next hill. Then leave the road and bear northwest uphill to the crest of the ridge.

The remainder of the hike is typical Mosquito Range ridge walking without an established trail. Mostly the ridge is broad and the footing secure, but there are some rocky sections, both up and down, where care is required and the going is slow.

Two and a half miles along the ridge bring you to the 13,614-foot summit of North Star Mountain. The high point is reached after

North Star Mountain from the highway south of Hoosier Pass. The climbing route follows the ridge to the high point at the extreme left.

two false summits are crossed with descents of 120 feet after each. This high point is three-quarters of a mile west of the name, "North Star Mountain" on the topographic map.

Along the ridge, and from the top, you can see Fourteeners Mount Lincoln to the south and Mount Democrat to the southwest, with their mines and 4WD roads. Quandary Peak, another Fourteener, dominates the view to the north. If you were to continue on the ridge beyond North Star Mountain, you would reach 13,690-foot Wheeler Mountain in another mile. The most spectacular view from the top of North Star is of the jagged ridge north from Wheeler, leading to 13,951-foot Fletcher Mountain. It's quite a contrast to the usual gentle Mosquito Range ridges.

To avoid all of the slow ridge and make a different return trip, you can follow a route that will take you by an interesting abandoned mine. Return about a mile along the ridge, over the first false summit to the next saddle, a point from where you can see the mine to the south about 350 feet below the ridge. Try to find a faint trail that leads off the ridge, and descend toward the visible mine buildings. Be sure to leave the mine exactly as you find it. New laws protect mine property.

After looking around the mine facilities, you may return along the old 4WD road as it contours on the south side of the ridge back to the saddle, one and one-half miles west of Hoosier Pass.

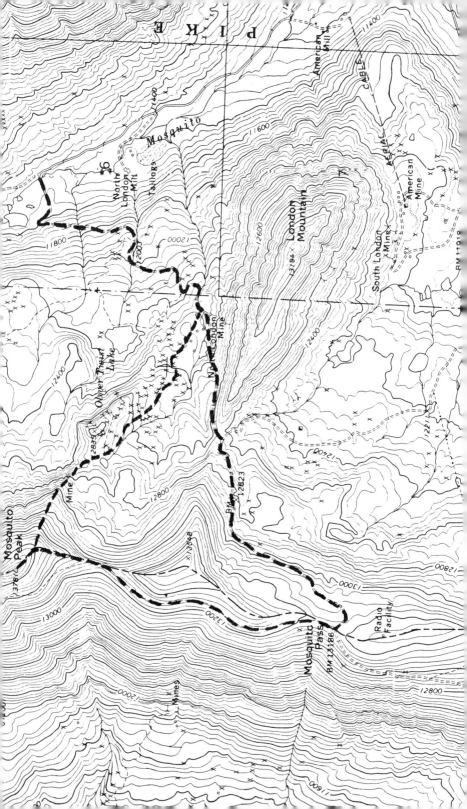

4. MOSQUITO PASS AND MOSQUITO PEAK

Distance: 6 miles (keyhole loop)
Starting elevation: 11,520 feet
High point: 13,781 feet
Elevation gain: 2,300 feet
Rating: moderate
Time allowed: 5 hours
Maps: 7.5 minute Climax
       Pike National Forest

Mosquito Pass, at 13,186 feet, is said to be the highest pass in North America crossed by a road. But what a road! You wouldn't want to attempt it except on a good day with a 4WD vehicle. However, you can get close enough to the pass with a regular car to make a fine hike, not only visiting the pass, but going by many interesting mines in the area and climbing a high peak as well.

The best approach is from the east. Take Colorado 9 for five miles north of Fairplay, and take a left fork at Alma Junction. Or from Breckenridge, go sixteen miles south on Colorado 9 to a road, Park County 10, leading west from the southern part of Alma. These roads join, after about two miles, at Park City. After another two and one-half miles, when you come to a fork in the road, take the right fork to head northwest in the valley east of London Mountain. Two and a half more miles take you to the head of the valley, where a road fork turns to the west over Mosquito Creek. This may be the parking place for regular cars, and the hike distance reflects this. Some cars may be able to proceed another mile west and southwest to the vicinity of North London Mine, perched on the north side of London Mountain.

From your parking place, walk on up the road for two miles, crossing a pass at 12,660 feet, west of London Mountain, and another mile to reach Mosquito Pass. From here you can survey the road leading to the west, which continues down to Leadville. If you happen to be there on the right day of the summer, you'll have lots of company watching the annual burro race from Leadville or Fairplay to Mosquito Pass and back.

Our hike continues to the north toward Mosquito Peak. There's a trail that bypasses the first false summit on the west side. It reaches a pass at 13,300 feet in about one mile. At this point, abandon the trail as it starts to contour around the west side of the peak, and head directly up the ridge to the summit.

From Mosquito Peak, at 13,781 feet, there's a good view of the Sawatch Range to the west, as well as of the basin to the east with its many mines.

There's an interesting descent route, somewhat more difficult but shorter than the route via Mosquito Pass. Head directly down the ridge to the southeast. This takes you by many mine diggings and leads to a trail that joins the road near North London Mine, from where you can return to your parking place.

5. PTARMIGAN PEAK AND WESTON PEAK

Distance: 3½ miles (out and back)
Starting elevation: 11,921 feet
High points: 13,739 and 13,572 feet
Elevation gain: 2,200 feet
Rating: moderate, because of the steep climb at the
    start
Time allowed: 5 hours
Maps: 7.5 minute Mount Sherman
        Pike National Forest
        San Isabel National Forest

This hike combines a drive to a scenic pass, a stiff climb to a ridge, and short walks along the ridge to two high points that provide striking views of the surrounding mountain ranges.

The starting point is at Weston Pass. This pass can either be reached from US 24 south of Leadville or from US 285 south of Fairplay. A good forest service road crosses the pass and offers the opportunity for a circle auto trip by approaching from one direction and leaving by another. If approaching from the east via Fairplay, the turnoff is five miles south on US 285. Another approach is off US 285 from the south, ten and one-half miles north of Antero Junction, the point where US 24 leaves US 285. These two approaches lead to a "T" from which a single road leads to Weston Pass. From the pass, the road proceeds in a northwesterly direction for eleven miles to emerge on US 24 seven miles south of Leadville. The eastern approach is usually better driving for regular cars, particularly in the early summer and in wet weather.

This hike is entirely off trail, but the country is open and the footing good, as it is entirely above timberline. The first part provides most of the climb—a disheartening feature for many hikers.

From Weston Pass, head up the slopes in a northeasterly direction. There's a climb of about 1,500 feet in a little less than a mile, so take it easy with frequent rests to view the Sawatch Range to the west. After reaching the ridge at 13,340 feet, head north along it toward Ptarmigan Peak. You can stay left of a 13,525-foot ridge

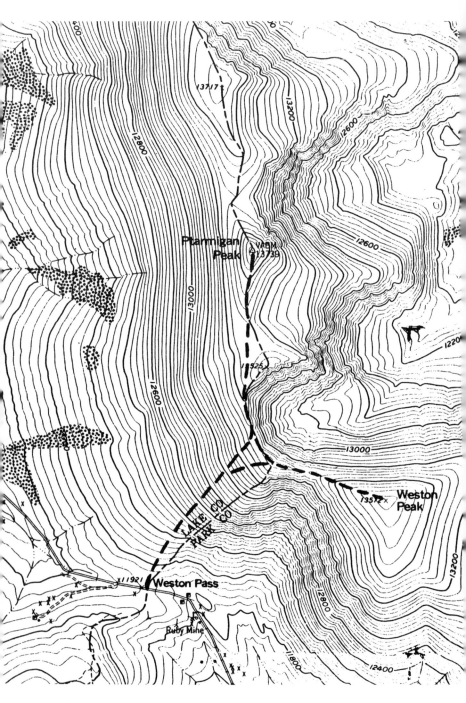

Ptarmigan
Peak

Weston
Peak

LAKE CO
PARK CO

Weston Pass

Ruby Mine

point, aiming for a flat area on the ridge before making the final climb to the peak. From the ridge and the peak, you can get a good view of South Park to the east and the mountain ranges beyond. Northward, the ridge continues for two and a half miles to Horseshoe Mountain at 13,898 feet. Beyond Horseshoe Mountain is 14,036-foot Mount Sherman, five miles away.

Return south along the ridge to the point that you reached when climbing from Weston Pass. Then continue to follow the ridge as it turns eastward. There are several minor ups and downs before you get to the final climb to Weston Peak. The last climb requires about 275 feet of elevation gain. Neither Ptarmigan Peak nor Weston Peak quite rate separate-mountain status on the criteria that a separate summit must be at least 300 feet above saddles between it and higher peaks. However, they both are interesting high points, well worth the effort to climb. For the return from Weston Peak, it's best not to try to come down the steep western slopes directly to Weston Pass. Follow the ridge westward until the slopes become more gentle before starting the descent.

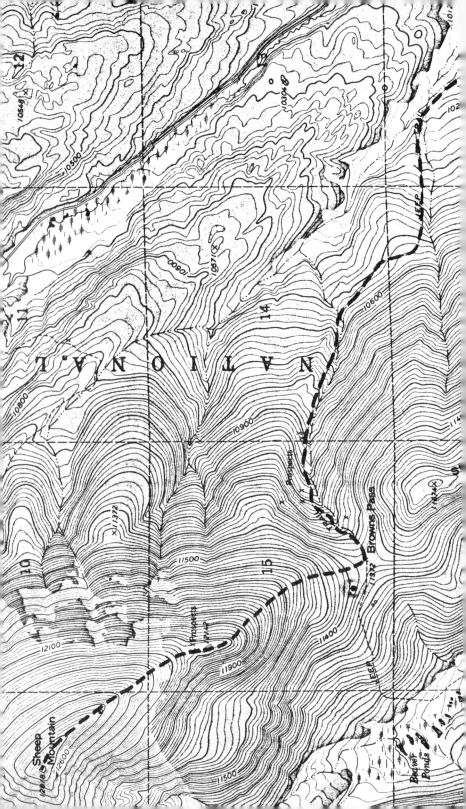

6. BROWNS PASS AND SHEEP MOUNTAIN

Distance: 9 miles (out and back)
Starting elevation: 10,000 feet
High point: 12,818 feet
Elevation gain: 2,900 feet
Rating: easy
Time allowed: 5 to 6 hours
Maps: 7.5 minute Fairplay West
  Pike National Forest

This hike combines a nice walk through the forest to a low pass, followed by an easy walk up a ridge to a low but isolated mountain summit. Sheep Mountain makes a good early or late season hike, since it is entirely in the protected forest and on a south-facing ridge.

To reach the trailhead, follow US 285 south three and one-half miles from the junction with Colorado 9 at Fairplay. Follow Park County 20, the unpaved road leading directly west. At two miles, take the right fork. This forest access road is a dirt track across a meadow, much less impressive than the left fork bearing southwest to Warm Springs Ranch. Three-quarters of a mile across the meadow brings you to the national forest boundary. Continue another half mile to another fork, where the left fork crosses a drainage. After this stream crossing, the road deteriorates. Therefore, consider this area the trailhead, and unless you want to drive further, find a place to park. Walk across the drainage and continue along the road to the northwest on the west side of the stream. After a brief stretch in the open, the road enters the forest.

The remaining two and a half miles to Browns Pass can be driven with 4WD or by some small cars, but this portion is interesting hiking through the forest and past mine diggings. Continue west, northwest, then west and southwest. You reach Browns Pass at 11,372 feet shortly after you enter an open area. The 4WD road continues west, down from Browns Pass. It reaches a long valley below and circles to the south around Sheep Ridge. It then turns southeast and reaches Break Neck Pass some two miles southeast of Browns Pass.

Sheep Mountain, with Browns Pass to the left, as viewed from the approach road across the meadow (above).
Dead wood along the trail to Browns Pass, with a view of South Park in the distance (below).

From Browns Pass, walk directly up the ridge to the north-northwest. The first mile, which involves a climb of about 800 feet, is through the timber. However, the country is relatively open, so walking is not difficult. There are a few old trails to help you along, but some lead off the ridge. Therefore, they should be avoided. Stay generally near the crest of the ridge for easiest walking.

After reaching open country at about 12,200 feet, continue along the ridge for a little less than a mile to the summit. In this portion there are some sections of trail. Many of these trails go around the mountain, so use only those that keep you near the crest of the ridge.

From the summit of 12,818-foot Sheep Mountain, the views are dramatic. Lower and to the west-southwest is the 12,438-foot Lamb Mountain. The direct route between Sheep Mountain and Lamb Mountain is quite rugged. Below, to the north, is the road, the entry to climb 14,036-foot Mount Sherman, which is four miles to the northwest. The impressive, large, horseshoe-shaped cirque of 13,898-foot Horseshoe Mountain stands out directly to the west. Since Sheep Mountain is on a ridge extending east from the crest of the Mosquito Range, the top affords an excellent panoramic view of South Park.

A shorter climb of Sheep Mountain can be made from the road, but it is much steeper and more difficult.

It's best to return the way that you came.

7. BUFFALO PASS AND
WEST BUFFALO PEAK

Distance: 14 miles (out and back)
Starting elevation: 9,220 feet
High point: 13,326 feet
Elevation gain: 4,200 feet
Rating: moderate but long, with lots of elevation gain
Time allowed: 10 hours
Maps: 7.5 minute Harvard Lakes
      7.5 minute Marmot Peak (peak area only)
      San Isabel National Forest

This hike provides a scenic walk along a creek through the forest, with many wild flowers in season. Then there's a steep trail to an interesting pass. From the pass, it's a climb up the ridge to the higher of the two Buffalo Peaks. The Buffalo Peaks stand alone as high points in South Park at the south end of the Mosquito Range.

There are two possible problems with this hike. First, it may be difficult for some cars to negotiate a portion of the road to the trailhead. Second, at times a section of the hike along Fourmile Creek, with its many beaver ponds, may be overrun with hoards of mosquitoes. If you meet these mosquitoes, you'll agree that the Mosquito Range is well named.

From the intersection of US 24 and Colorado 306 in Buena Vista, go east to Colorado Avenue, the second street beyond the railroad crossing. Turn north-northwest on a paved road, which turns to gravel before it crosses the Arkansas River at 2.0 miles. At 2.6 miles, take the right fork up the hill on the Fourmile Creek road, rather than entering the old railroad tunnel straight ahead.

The next mile of road is somewhat rough in the steep sections, particularly if it hasn't been graded recently, but most cars can make it readily. Once past this mile, the remainder of the road to the trailhead is better. Keep left, over a cattle guard at a junction at 3.7 miles. The rougher portion of the road passes some weird but interesting rock formations.

The Buffalo Peaks as seen from a ridge off the road to the trailhead. East Buffalo Peak is on the right, the higher West Buffalo Peak is in the center, and the hiking route up the ridge may be seen on the left.

Continue on the most traveled road, avoiding turnoffs to camping and picnic spots, mines, and ranch properties. At 7.9 miles, the Fourmile Creek road makes a sharp turn to the right with a gradual descent, while an equally prominent road continues straight ahead up the hill. The uphill road crosses the ridge and dead-ends after three miles. It gives impressive views of the Sawatch Range but is no help in getting to Buffalo Pass.

After the right turn at the junction, one more mile brings you to the trailhead. This parking area at 9,220 feet may be recognized by a faint track continuing straight ahead in a level area while the road turns left up the hill.

With 4WD, the road might be negotiated another mile and a half. This section is mostly good road, but drainage crossings and steep rough sections stop most regular cars.

From the parking area, walk up the 4WD road. After about a half mile, take the left fork up the hill, since the right fork dead-ends in about a quarter mile. Another mile on the 4WD road brings you to a barrier stopping all vehicles. Continue on the track straight ahead, which becomes an excellent trail leading down to the creek. The next mile of trail stays on the left side of Fourmile Creek, giving a very scenic walk, particularly when the creek is full in the early summer.

The trail crosses to the east side of the creek and enters a flat area. Numerous old beaver dams, some quite large, form successive ponds as you proceed along the creek. The trail continues to follow Fourmile Creek closely. It crosses to the west side of the creek, and as it leaves the flat area, in the dark forest, a steep ascent begins. Finally, reaching more open country, switchbacks bring you the remaining distance to unofficially named Buffalo Pass, which is at 11,420 feet.

From the pass, walk directly east through the open forest. In this area, along with mosquitoes, we once flushed out ruffed grouse. Soon you'll reach open slopes, so continue east toward the 12,917-foot false summit, which is northwest of West Buffalo Peak.

Until late summer, a large snowbank sits west of West Buffalo Peak and east of this false summit. This snowbank may be difficult to cross, since it is rather steep. Therefore, it's better to bypass it if possible. Once around or over the snowbank, it is a direct climb to the summit.

From the top of 13,326-foot West Buffalo Peak, the views are impressive, as you would expect from such an isolated summit. Across the Arkansas River to the west is an array of Fourteeners extending from Mount Shavano northward, including Mount Antero and the Collegiate Peaks of Princeton, Yale, Columbia, Harvard, and Oxford. A mile to the east is the 13,300-foot East Buffalo Peak, with a low point of about 12,800 feet in between. You may want to include East Buffalo Peak in this hike. If so, that'll add another two miles and 1,000 feet of elevation gain.

Whether or not you've included East Buffalo Peak in this day's outing, it's best to return to Buffalo Pass and follow the trail back the way you came.

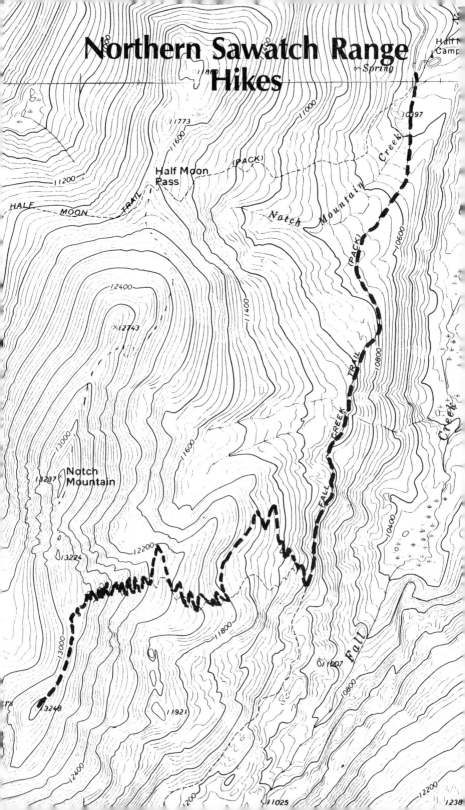

Northern Sawatch Range Hikes

8. NOTCH MOUNTAIN

> *Distance: 11 miles (out and back)*
> *Starting elevation: 10,300 feet*
> *High point: 13,248 feet*
> *Elevation gain: 3,000 feet*
> *Rating: easy trail, but moderate if you go to the*
> *   13,248-foot high point*
> *Time allowed: 9 hours*
> *Maps: 7.5 minute Mount of the Holy Cross*
> *   7.5 minute Minturn (trailhead only)*
> *   White River National Forest*

This is a popular hike to a well-known destination, the best place for viewing the cross on Mount of the Holy Cross. It's on good trail all the way. If you want to go to the high point of the mountain, it's then a bit of a rocky walk on top.

On US 24, drive two miles south of Minturn or thirty-one miles north of Leadville to a road leading west to Half Moon Campground. Eight miles on this sometimes rough road brings you to a parking area at the road's end just beyond the entrance to the campground.

Two trails lead south from this parking area. The one to the right goes to Half Moon Pass. The left one is to Lake Constantine and Fall Creek Pass, which is the one we follow to Notch Mountain. Two miles on this trail brings you to a junction. Here you leave the Lake Constantine trail, turn right, and head up the trail to Notch Mountain.

There's nothing hard about the next three miles of trail, but two thousand feet of climbing are involved. You can while away the time by counting the number of switchbacks—we lost count after getting to thirty or forty. One switchback takes you to the edge of the ridge, from which you can get a good view of the inside of the notch for which Notch Mountain is named.

Finally, you reach a flat area and a shelter cabin and can look across to the west and see Mount of the Holy Cross. If you're here at the right time of year, you can see the optimum amount of snow that forms the cross. In any event, one arm is eroded away more than shown in pictures taken years ago. Even without snow, you can pick out the huge cross on the face of the mountain.

Mount of the Holy Cross from Notch Mountain. (photo by Bill Bueler)

At this point you're south of the notch, and the topographic map shows Notch Mountain to be a 13,237-foot high point north of the notch, a half mile away. Then there's a 13,224-foot point midway between, just south of the notch. That's a good one to climb to get a view of the notch. However, the high point of the entire Notch Mountain massif is the 13,248-foot point a half mile to the south. Whether this is really the summit of Notch Mountain or a separate summit is open to question.

Assuming that you want to visit the 13,248-foot high point, it's a slow walk over the rocks. A couple of hundred feet of elevation need to be gained. When you get there, you'll find little evidence that very many people who climb to the Notch Mountain viewpoint also climb this high point.

The map seems to indicate that a good circle trip would be to cross the notch to the named Notch Mountain summit, head down the ridge to the north to Half Moon Pass, and return to the starting point by the trail from there. However, because of the extreme difficulty in crossing the notch, we don't recommend this route, so we've written up this hike to return by the way you came.

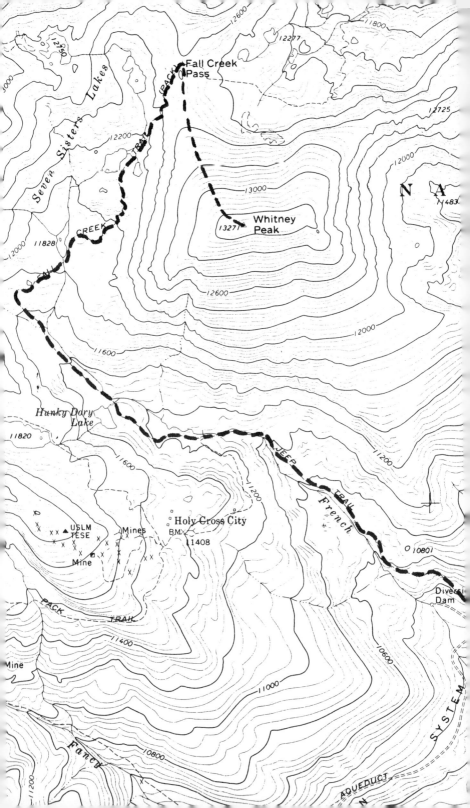

9. SEVEN SISTERS LAKES, FALL CREEK PASS, AND WHITNEY PEAK

Distance: 12 miles (out and back)
Starting elevation: 10,280 feet
High point: 13,271 feet
Elevation gain: 3,200 feet
Rating: moderate
Time allowed: 8 to 9 hours
Maps: 7.5 minute Mount of the Holy Cross
White River National Forest

This hike combines a walk along a rugged 4WD road, a beautiful trail passing by a number of lakes, a climb to a pass, and a walk up gentle slopes to a high peak. There are good views of the Holy Cross Ridge, a string of high summits extending south from Mount of the Holy Cross.

The trailhead is reached from the Homestake Reservoir road, which leads north from US 24 between Leadville and Minturn. Go nine and one-half miles north of Tennessee Pass or ten miles south of Minturn on US 24 to a gravel road leading west at the base of a sharp "S" curve. Follow this unpaved road, which is the Homestake Reservoir road, for seven miles to the entrance to Gold Park Campground. A mile farther, turn right on road 704 and drive generally west and southwest for two miles. At a "T" turn right, and go north for almost two miles to the end of the auto road at 10,280 feet. At a junction after one mile, keep right and go a little downhill instead of following a switchback to the left up the hill. Park in a level area where the road continues uphill to the left and a 4WD road leads straight ahead.

Walk up the 4WD road which, within fifty yards, meets another road coming up the hill. Follow this road, which in part is a test for the best 4WD vehicles, for about a mile and a half. At a large flat area, another 4WD road goes uphill, to the left, toward Holy Cross City. At this point, continue on the road circling the meadow on the south. Beyond the meadow, the road climbs somewhat before reaching Hunky Dory Lake.

Meadow below Hunky Dory Lake on the route to Fall Creek Pass.

You may prefer to cut directly across the meadow on any of several faint trails and vehicle tracks. However, the advantage of this shortcut through the flowers and green meadow may be offset by the boggy conditions underfoot.

From Hunky Dory Lake, a good trail climbs along the west side of French Creek and then reaches the Seven Sisters Lakes area. In this section, the trail weaves around several of the lakes in picturesque patterns. Here you get good views of the Holy Cross Ridge, with its rugged cliffs to the west.

Continue along the excellent trail, with several minor creek crossings, to reach Fall Creek Pass at 12,580 feet. From the pass, the trail continues down into the Fall Creek valley. It passes Lake Constantine and eventually reaches the Half Moon Campground, the starting point for the hike to Notch Mountain (hike number 8).

Our route from Fall Creek Pass is up the ridge to Whitney Peak, toward the south-southeast. The total climb from the pass to the top is about 800 feet. The grade is gentle and the walking is not difficult. If rests are needed, the views of Holy Cross Ridge are worth a few stops.

First you must climb over or around a rocky point just south of the pass. Then the walking is mostly on tundra, which is ablaze

46

Looking south, back along the trail, from Fall Creek Pass.

with flowers in the early summer. As the route goes higher, it becomes more rocky.

Continuing upward along the rounded ridge brings you to a summit point marked by a benchmark, indicating the 13,271-foot point shown on the USGS topographic map. But is this the top? To the east, a quarter mile away, is a point that appears to be higher. It's an easy walk over the almost-level terrain to that summit, which is topped by a large block boulder.

From this point, a look back may still leave you guessing as to which is the true summit.

Whitney Peak, because of its isolated location, offers good views in all directions. The Gore Range, Mosquito Range, parts of the Front Range, and the Elks, in addition to the nearby Holy Cross Ridge and Notch Mountain, are plainly in view.

While the southeast ridge would appear to be a good descent route, the scenic nature of your trip to the top should make you want to return the way you came. One minor variation would be to avoid the rocky point just south of Fall Creek Pass and drop down on the left to the main trail, using any of several game trails on the grassy slopes.

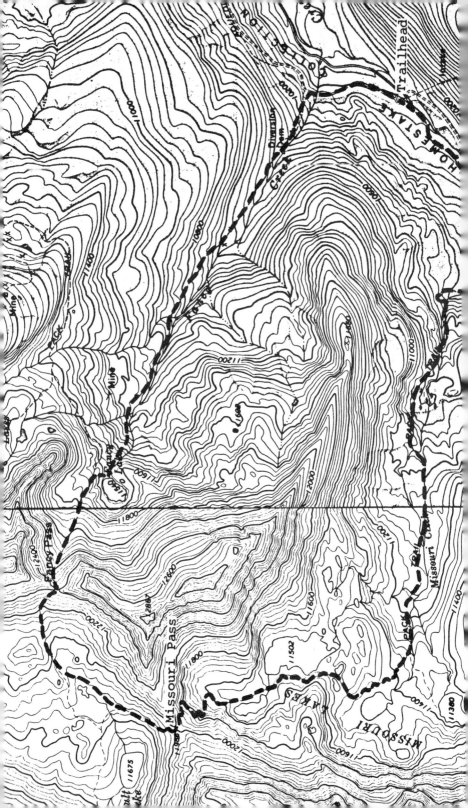

10. FANCY PASS AND MISSOURI PASS LOOP

Distance: 10 miles (loop)
Starting elevation: 10,020 feet
High point: 12,380 feet
Elevation gain: 2,550 feet
Rating: moderate
Time allowed: 6 to 7 hours
Maps: 7.5 minute Mount of the Holy Cross
7.5 minute Mount Jackson
White River National Forest

This is one of the best loop trips in the area. You follow a trail to a scenic lake, then cross a pass to the head of a beautiful valley, walk through the valley to another pass, and return on an excellent trail by a series of scenic lakes. This trip is best taken in the late summer or early fall, after most of the snows are gone and the colors are at their height.

To reach the trailhead, follow the route described in hike number 9, Seven Sisters Lakes, Fall Creek Pass, and Whitney Peak. When you reach the "T," at 10,020 feet, park there. At the "T," you'll be at a point where the Fancy Pass trail is to the right and the Missouri Pass trail is to the left.

Walk up the road to the right, or north, for a half mile. Just beyond a crossing of Fancy Creek, there's a 4WD road leading up the hill steeply to the left. Follow this road, which becomes a trail beyond a diversion dam. Continue on this trail along the northeast side of Fancy Creek. A bit of route finding is necessary across a meadow and then again as the trail winds through some rocky areas. Continue on to reach Fancy Lake, at an elevation of 11,540 feet, about two miles from the trailhead.

Fancy Lake is set in a rugged cirque backed by a high ridge. Circle to the right, to the north side of the lake. You then need to make a short, steep climb up a gully to the north of the lake. This brings you to the old road that leads from Holy Cross City to Fancy Pass. Turn left on this old road and continue on to Fancy Pass.

Snowbanks remain in the cirque east of Fancy Pass until late in the summer, so it may be necessary to do some climbing over the

Waterfall along the trail below Missouri Lakes.

snow to reach the pass. From Fancy Pass, you then look down into the upper Cross Creek valley. The nearby lake is Treasure Vault Lake, while the large one across the valley is Blodgett Lake.

The route crosses the Holy Cross Ridge at Fancy Pass and will recross it at Missouri Pass. Continue down the trail toward Treasure Vault Lake. It's possible to avoid some elevation loss by leaving the trail and crossing the flat area to rejoin the trail as it approaches Missouri Pass to the southwest. In any case, the climb to the pass is short. Missouri Pass, at 11,986 feet, is not officially named, but there used to be a picturesque old sign proclaiming it to be Missouri Pass.

From Missouri Pass, it's a scenic descent into the Missouri Creek basin. The trail winds beside the several Missouri Lakes and then heads on down Missouri Creek. There are impressive cliffs in the lower part of the creek basin. After several creek crossings on good bridges and beyond a diversion dam, there's a trail leading off to the left as you get in sight of the aqueduct road. The trail to the left makes a better return route to the starting point than a walk down the road.

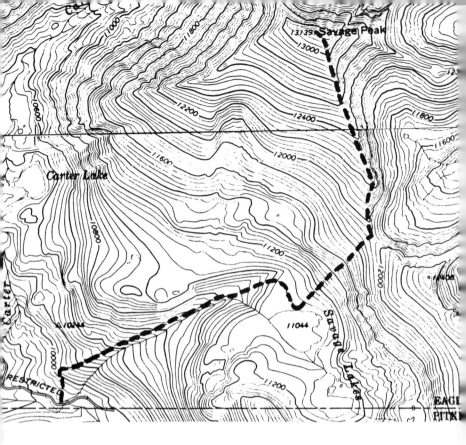

11. SAVAGE LAKE AND SAVAGE PEAK

Distance: 8 miles (out and back)
Starting elevation: 9,880 feet
High point: 13,139 feet
Elevation gain: 3,300 feet
Rating: moderate
Time allowed: 7 or 8 hours
Maps: 7.5 minute Nast
7.5 minute Mount Jackson
White River National Forest

This fine trip follows a very scenic trail through the forest along-side a winding stream. After reaching a picturesque lake, there's a walk up tundra slopes to a pass along the Holy Cross Ridge. Then it's a climb up the ridge to Savage Peak, the southernmost high point on that rugged ridge.

From Basalt, on Colorado 82 between Aspen and Glenwood Springs, drive east twenty-seven miles on a paved road to a point two miles beyond Thomasville. You also can reach Thomasville from Interstate 70 on a somewhat lesser quality road by going south through Eagle and crossing Crooked Creek Pass. This is a scenic drive, especially in the fall because of the aspen-covered hillsides and the varied-colored rocks. A 4WD-only route to the point near Thomasville, from the east, is out of Leadville and over Hagerman Pass.

Two miles southeast of Thomasville, take the road directly east past the Elk Wallow Campground. From the turnoff, it's seven miles to the trailhead. Take the left fork after four miles. The trailhead can be identified as being a half mile beyond an ''S''-curve. There's a wide parking area near the crossing of Savage Creek.

Follow the excellent trail that leads off on the north side of the road on the west side of Savage Creek. The trail climbs, sometimes steeply, through the forest as it remains on the northwest side of the creek. As you approach Savage Lake, the grade becomes more gradual and you enter some marshy areas with additional side trails. However, the route to the lake can be easily followed through the timber.

You can look across the large lower lake and see the basin that holds the upper Savage Lake to the southeast. Our route turns to the northeast. Make your way through the timber in that direction, staying left of the cliffs east of Savage Lake. Soon you leave the trees to break out in the open on the tundra and grassy slope. Continue northeast, making for a pass at 11,940 feet.

This unnamed pass gives you a view of the valley on the east side of the Holy Cross Ridge. The route to Savage Peak is up the ridge to the left. This involves a climb of 1,200 feet in about a mile, but the grade is consistent and the footing is good.

From Savage Peak, you can look down to the northeast at the Missouri Lakes and the Missouri Creek basin. After absorbing these views, return the way that you came.

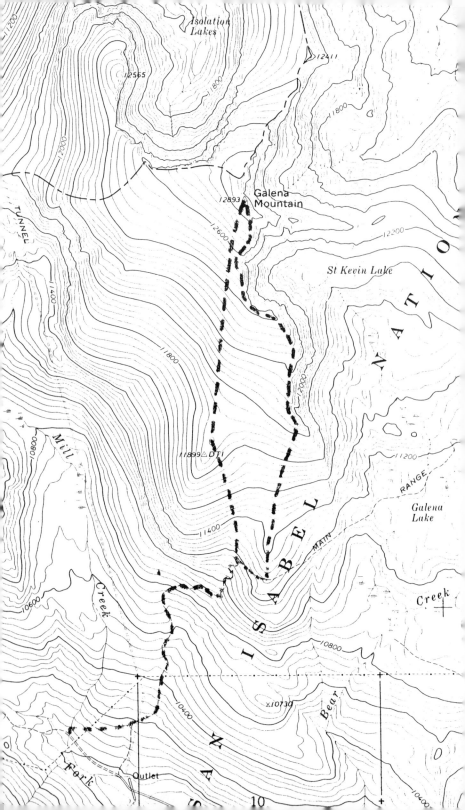

12. GALENA MOUNTAIN

Distance: 7 miles (keyhole loop)
Starting elevation: 9,960 feet
High point: 12,893 feet
Elevation gain: 2,950 feet
Rating: easy
Time allowed: 7 hours
Maps: 7.5 minute Homestake Reservoir
San Isabel National Forest

As you drive north toward Leadville on US 24, the highest peaks are Mount Elbert and Mount Massive on your left. However, the most rugged looking mountain is the one straight ahead. That's Galena Mountain. While the side you see from the highway is impressive, with near-vertical cliffs, Galena Mountain offers an easy and interesting route to the summit.

The trailhead is at Turquoise Lake, west of Leadville. Follow the scenic paved road around either side of this large lake. Continue to the extreme west end of the lake to a small parking area on the west side of the road, at the point where the road loops back to the east.

Cross the creek just west of the parking place and hike north a hundred yards up the west side of the creek. The trail starts with a bridge crossing back to the east side of the creek.

The scenic trail climbs through the forest, across streams, and through meadows. It leads into an open area, climbing on switchbacks to an 11,300-foot saddle on the south ridge of Galena Mountain. At this saddle, leave the trail and head up the ridge to the north. This gentle ridge can be followed all the way to the summit. If you carefully approach the edge to the east, you can look down the steep cliffs that are visible from the road. The Galena Mountain summit is on the Continental Divide. From the summit, you can trace the divide winding to the west and looping back south to the west side of Mount Massive. The Continental Divide extends north to Homestake Peak, three and one-half miles away, before turning to the east.

A slight variation can be followed on the descent. Come down from the top of Galena Mountain west of the ascent route to visit a

Galena Mountain from the highway south of Leadville.

small knoll at 11,920 feet. From here it is an easy descent south into the valley somewhat west of the ascent route, and back to the trail.

In the early summer, this hike is best for the beauty of the streams, meadows, and forests. Unfortunately, that's also the most likely time to run into hoards of mosquitoes, so be prepared.

New roads have been built and trails rerouted in this area since the USGS 7.5 minute Homestake Reservoir quadrangle was issued in 1970. The road reaches a point about a mile west of the road end shown on the USGS map, and a new road around the north side of the lake has been built. The Main Range Trail has been rerouted to reach the western extension of the road from its previous location to the east.

If the creek is flowing too full for an easy crossing to the west side from your parking place, you may follow faint paths north along the east side of the creek to intersect the trail.

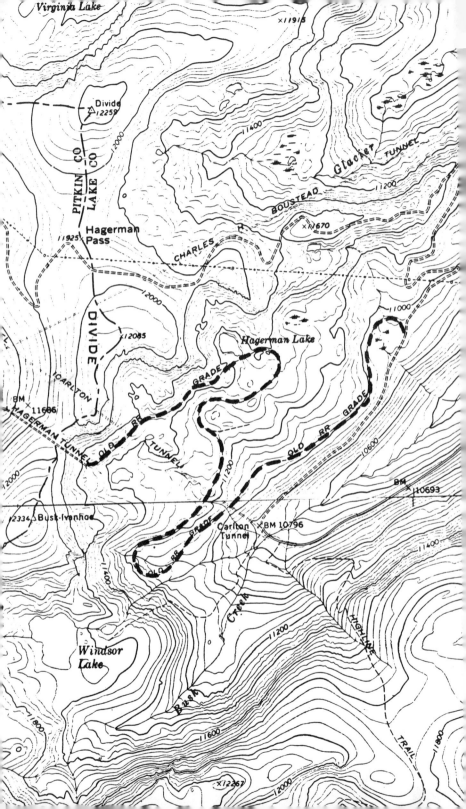

13. RAILROAD GRADE TO HAGERMAN TUNNEL

Distance: 6 miles (out and back)
Starting elevation: 10,940 feet
High point: 11,560 feet
Elevation gain: 800 feet
Rating: easy
Time allowed: 4 hours
Maps: 7.5 minute Homestake Reservoir
7.5 minute Mount Massive (barely on the edge)
San Isabel National Forest

While this is one of the easiest hikes covered, it is without doubt one of the most interesting. It takes you along the route of a railroad that crossed the Continental Divide through a tunnel. Interesting remains of the railroad make the hike an historic trek. You will need to visualize some of the essentials of the railroad grade that are no longer there, because portions of the original route are missing.

The trailhead is on the Hagerman Pass road. From Leadville, follow the road west on the south side of Turquoise Lake. After passing by most of the lake, take the left fork at the "Y" junction. This unpaved road heads directly west, then turns to the south to circle a vast basin.

As the road makes a sharp turn to the right, you come upon the east portal of the old Carlton Tunnel. This is worth a stop to peer into the dark and wet interior, but don't go in.

Drive another mile on the road, which now curves around to head northeast. Our trailhead is on the left, and there's a large parking area on the right side of the road.

At one time there was a large sign at the trailhead that explained the history of the railroad. Hopefully, it'll still be there. Walk up the railroad grade, now a 4WD road supposedly closed to vehicles, to the northwest through a narrow-sided gully. The route soon curves to the south and leaves the gully for more open country.

After following the route to the south and southwest, you come to a place where the route can't continue at the railroad grade level. This is the area where there was once a large, curved trestle

Sign at the start of the trail to Hagerman Tunnel.

to carry the tracks around a curve and back toward the northeast. Try to visualize how the trestle once carried the rails around the curve to the grade above. You should make a sharp right turn on an old road and follow it to the railroad grade above.

There's another missing trestle as you approach the curve to the northeast, in the vicinity of Hagerman Lake. Turning back toward the southwest, the railroad grade leads to the portal of Hagerman Tunnel. As you approach the tunnel, look for the timbers that were part of a snowshed that collapsed long ago.

Hagerman Tunnel was the original tunnel in this area, carrying a standard gauge railroad. It was later replaced by the Carlton Tunnel that you passed on the road below the trailhead. Hagerman Tunnel

Old railroad grade, which is the trail to Hagerman Tunnel.

is not blocked off, but it is never safe to enter such tunnels. However, it is difficult to enter in any case because of fallen rock, and the tunnel is usually filled with snow.

There are some shortcuts that can be taken to return to the trailhead, but following the railroad grade is the recommended route.

Reaching the trailhead for this hike requires four and one-half miles of driving on an unpaved road. This drive seems much longer because the road is, in places, rocky, narrow, and often wet. There is a precipitous drop off on one side for most of the distance. However, it can usually be negotiated by regular cars.

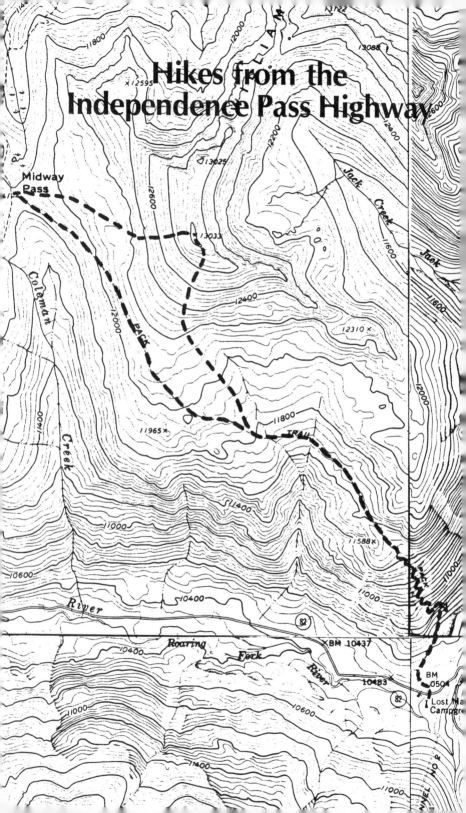

Hikes from the
Independence Pass Highway

14. PEAK 13,033, WILLIAMS MOUNTAINS, AND MIDWAY PASS

Distance: 7½ miles (keyhole loop)
Starting elevation: 10,500 feet
High point: 13,033 feet
Elevation gain: 3,000 feet
Rating: easy, but with substantial elevation gain
Time allowed: 6 to 7 hours
Maps: 7.5 minute Thimble Rock

> *7.5 minute Independence Pass (shows start of hike but only first 0.3 mile)*

> *7.5 minute Mount Champion (0.5 mile through corner)*
> *White River National Forest*

This hike is unique in two respects. First, it takes you on the one easy approach to a 13,000-foot summit in the rugged Williams Mountains. The Williams Mountains, with five separate summits over 13,000 feet, is one of the most scenic and least visited areas. These mountains lie just west of the Sawatch Range. Second, on most hikes to passes, the pass is approached from below so that the panorama on the other side unfolds all at once. In this hike, you have already seen the other side from the mountain above. You come down to the pass.

The trailhead is on Colorado 82, fourteen miles east of Aspen or six miles west of Independence Pass. Drive to the Lost Man Parking Area, which is on the north side of the highway across from Lost Man Campground. This trailhead serves both the Midway Pass and Lost Man Creek trails.

From the trailhead parking area, hike west and north to a trail junction. Take the left fork and follow the excellent trail as it switchbacks up the hillside to the west. After a mile or so, the grade decreases as the trail straightens out through the forest. Soon you'll reach an open area, as you leave the timber, where the gentle slope of the mountain to the north can be seen. Look for an easy place to leave the trail and plod up the open slope.

Buildings at the ghost town of Independence near the start of the trail to Midway Pass.

Upon reaching the top of Peak 13,033, you can look down the ridge to the north toward the other more rugged peaks of the Williams Mountains. More spectacular is the view of the Elk Range to the southwest. You should have no trouble identifying the Maroon Bells and Snowmass Mountain.

To the west is Midway Pass, at 11,841 feet. It is the low point between Peak 13,033 and the 12,921-foot unnamed summit to the west. Head down the slope on easy footing directly toward Midway Pass and the trail that crosses it. From the pass, the trail leading north is into the Midway Creek valley—good backpacking country.

Our hike takes us from Midway Pass on the trail to the south, which requires a climb of 300 feet to reach a high point on the south flank of Peak 13,033. Shortly beyond is the point where you originally left the trail, and the route back from here is the same one followed on the ascent.

15. SOUTH FORK PASS AND PEAK 13,203, WILLIAMS MOUNTAINS

Distance: 10 miles (out and back)
Starting elevation: 10,500 feet
High point: 13,203 feet
Elevation gain: 3,000 feet
Rating: difficult because of the rugged final quarter
  mile to the summit
Time allowed: 8 hours
Maps: 7.5 minute Independence Pass
  7.5 minute Mount Champion
  White River National Forest

This varied hike combines an interesting and scenic trail, a climb of a broad ridge to near the objective, and then a testy scramble up the rocks to the summit. The Williams Mountains are a western extension from the northern part of the Sawatch Range, north of the Independence Pass road. They contain some of the most rugged summits in the area. There are five separate summits above 13,000 feet and six more in the 12,000-foot class. The highest is 13,382 feet. None are named. Perhaps because of this fact and since none of the summits are as high as many mountains in the general area, the Williams Mountains are practically neglected as climbing objectives.

While the hike rates as difficult because of the final portion, those wishing an easier hike can enjoy a fine all-trail route by going only as far as South Fork Pass. A hike to the pass is a round-trip of seven miles with an elevation gain of 1,300 feet.

The trailhead is the same as for hike number 14. Drive to the Lost Man Parking Area north of Colorado 82 almost six miles west of Independence Pass.

Hike along the trail west and north to a junction. At the trail junction, choose the right fork that takes you north along the west side of Lost Man Reservoir. For about a mile the trail is through the meadows with little gain in elevation. It then enters the forest, always staying on the west side of Lost Man Creek. After another mile or so, the trail becomes a little steeper as it climbs toward South Fork Pass.

For about a mile the trail is through the meadows with little gain in elevation. It then enters the forest, always staying on the

Trail along the stream from Lost Man Reservoir, near the start of the hike to South Fork Pass.

west side of Lost Man Creek. After another mile or so, the trail becomes a little steeper as it climbs toward South Fork Pass.

After reaching the junction of the trail leading right toward Lost Man Lake, another quarter of a mile brings you to South Fork Pass. The trail continues on down into Deadman Gulch to the north.

The route to the mountain leads up a broad open ridge to the west from South Fork Pass. Follow the easiest route up this ridge. There is no trail, but the country is open, and route-finding should be no problem. Peak 13,203, our objective, can be seen just to the right of this ridge. To the north of it is a spectacular ridge with a large cleft that leads to Peak 13,382, the highest point in the Williams Mountains. Continue up-ridge until you reach a small rounded knoll, which is at 13,100 feet. From this point, Peak 13,203, our objective, is directly to the north, only a hundred feet higher and a quarter mile away.

Lost Man Reservoir in early June. The trail to South Fork Pass proceeds up the valley beyond.

The remainder of the climb looks much harder than it really is. However, it is an interesting rock scramble and is the only section that gives this hike a rating of "difficult."

After an easy descent of about 120 feet along the ridge, approach the first rocky section on the left, or west, of the large rock towers. Beyond these obstacles, bear right to the top of the ridge. For the remainder of the climb, seek the easiest route either on the ridge or somewhat east of the ridge top. When the peak is reached, the views are spectacular. You will have the satisfaction of having climbed to a summit where few climbers have been.

Take time to admire the flowers and streams in this beautiful country as you return. It is not necessary to go all the way back to South Fork Pass as you come off the ridge. You can shorten the return by heading for a point on the trail somewhat south of the pass.

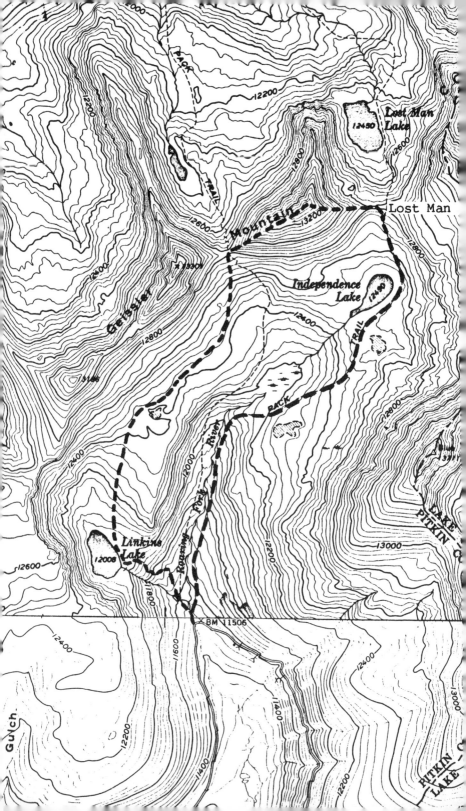

16. LOST MAN PASS AND EAST GEISSLER MOUNTAIN

Distance: 5 miles (loop)
Starting elevation: 11,506 feet
High point: 13,380 feet
Elevation gain: 1,900 feet
Rating: moderate, but short
Time allowed: 5 hours
Maps: 7.5 minute Mount Champion
      7.5 minute Independence Pass
      White River National Forest

This hike up a beautiful valley takes you by a large scenic lake, reaches an interesting pass, and ascends a mountain that overlooks valleys in all directions.

The trailhead is at the first hairpin curve on Colorado 82 two miles west of Independence Pass. It is twenty-six miles west of US 24, or eighteen miles east of Aspen. A parking area is provided north of the highway.

The route follows the Roaring Fork River to the north. It is important to get on the trail that goes up the east side of the river. Avoid the trail on the west side and a fork of it that bears off to the left up the hill toward Linkins Lake. The objective is to stay east of the drainage all the way to Independence Lake at 12,490 feet. Go around Independence Lake and head for the pass directly north. Although the topographic map shows a trail on the east side of the lake, this trail is sketchy, at best. It may be easier to follow a cairned route on the west side of the lake, although no trails are needed in this open country. Lost Man Pass, at 12,820 feet, is not named on the topographic map but is commonly referred to by that name.

From the pass, the even larger Lost Man Lake can be seen to the north. Also notice the continuation of the trail down Lost Man Creek before starting up East Geissler Mountain.

Geissler Mountain has two separate summits. The eastern one, the highest, and the one that we will climb on this hike, is 13,380 feet, or just 560 feet higher than the pass. Walk directly up the ridge westward from the pass. The rocks make for slow going, but the distance is short. From the peak, there is a good view of valleys

Geissler Mountain from Linkins Lake. (photo by Gordon McKeague)

Approaching the west summit of Geissler Mountain. (photo by Gordon McKeague)

in all directions. Just across Lost Man Pass, to the east, is the Continental Divide ridge, running south to north, then swinging to the east beyond Lost Man Lake.

Our route continues from the east summit of Geissler Mountain down the ridge to the west to reach the 12,820-foot saddle between the two summits of Geissler Mountain. From that point, there is a choice of routes. If you're inclined to climb the West Geissler Mountain summit, it's a short half mile away and less than 500 feet higher, at 13,301 feet.

If you climb West Geissler Mountain, return to the pass between the two summits. A visit to Linkins Lake from the pass between the Geissler Mountain summits can be made by following the flat area to the southwest. From Linkins Lake, a well-worn trail leads back to the trailhead. If time is limited, the shortest way back is directly south from the pass to meet the trail along the west side of the Roaring Fork River.

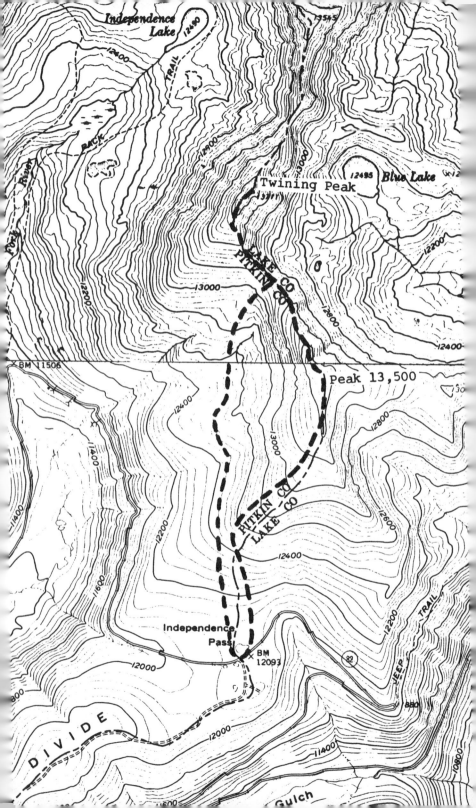

17. INDEPENDENCE PASS TO PEAK 13,500 AND TWINING PEAK

Distance: 4 miles (keyhole loop)
Starting elevation: 12,093 feet
High point: 13,711 feet
Elevation gain: 2,000 feet
Rating: moderate, short, but all at high altitude
Time allowed: 4 hours
Maps: 7.5 minute Independence Pass
7.5 minute Mount Champion
San Isabel National Forest
White River National Forest

Ridge walking from Independence Pass, the highest paved-road pass in the state, is good in either direction. Most tourists that are casual hikers opt to walk along the easy ridge to the south. However, the ridge to the north offers more interesting climbing, two separate summits, and two of the highest peaks that can be reached in a short distance from a major highway.

Independence Pass, at 12,093 feet, is on Colorado 82 about twenty miles east of Aspen and twenty-four miles west of US 24. There's a large parking area at the pass. Walk directly north, staying to the right of a marshy area, and head up the slopes. Bear somewhat to the left of the visible high point, then head to the right on the easier terrain. Pick the best route through tundra and over the rocks north to the summit of unnamed Peak 13,500. This summit gives an excellent view of the country south of Independence Pass.

The route to Twining Peak is along the Continental Divide ridge to the north. This involves a drop of 360 feet and a climb of 570 feet in slightly less than a mile. The best route is generally along the top of the ridge. Recently named Twining Peak, at 13,711 feet, is shown as a USGS benchmark, "Blue," on older topographic maps.

These two peaks offer excellent views of the Elks and the southern Sawatch. You can see the continuation of the Continental Divide as it goes north, then east and north again.

An interesting and easier variation can be followed on the return. Go back to the 13,140-foot saddle between the two peaks. Then head down to the west to a more level area some 600 feet below. Contour and descend slightly to the west of Peak 13,500, staying well above the steep slopes above the highway to the west. Continue to within sight of Independence Pass. From here it's easy walking back down to the starting point.

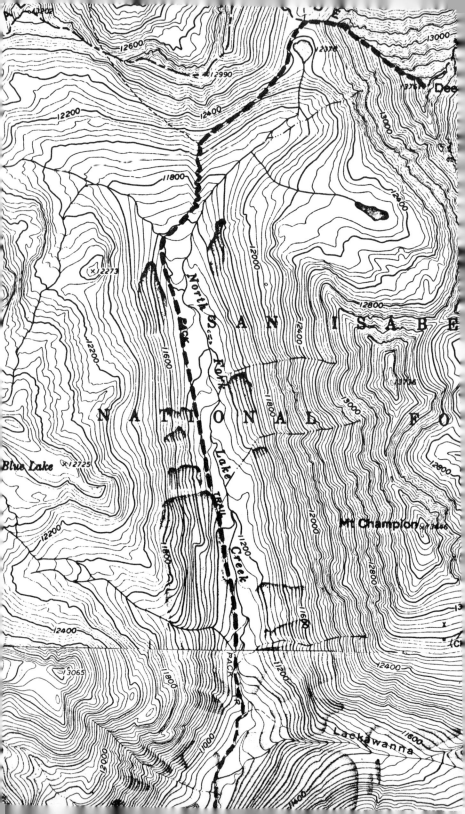

18. DEER MOUNTAIN

Distance: 9 miles (out and back)
Starting elevation: 10,794 feet
High point: 13,761 feet
Elevation gain: 3,000 feet
Rating: moderate
Time allowed: 8 hours
Maps: 7.5 minute Independence Pass
      7.5 minute Mount Champion
      San Isabel National Forest
      White River National Forest

This moderately strenuous trek starts at a highway, takes a trail up a scenic valley to an interesting pass, and follows a rough ridge to a high 13,000-foot peak.

The trailhead is at the first hairpin curve on the Independence Pass road when approaching from the east side of the pass. Take Colorado 82 for nineteen miles west of US 24, five miles east of Independence Pass, or twenty-five miles east of Aspen. At the hairpin curve at 10,794 feet, an unpaved road leads north from just east of this curve, offering good parking space. Walk up this 4WD road leading north, which turns into a trail after a half mile.

The trail leads north on the west side of the North Fork Lake Creek. After a couple of miles it becomes less distinct and more difficult to follow in the multitude of sheep trails from past intensive grazing. The route is along the drainage to the northeast. Stay generally north of the drainage for best walking. Another mile in the open valley brings you to an unnamed lake at 12,378 feet and then to an unnamed pass at 12,460 feet. From this pass you can see north into the Fryingpan River valley.

Deer Mountain is only about a mile up the ridge to the east, but it is 1,300 feet above the pass. So from an altitude-gained standpoint, the hike is just over half done. The ridge is slow going but not really difficult. The top of the ridge generally offers the best route, so stay as close to it as possible.

From the top, the ridge to the northeast leading to 13,845-foot Mount Oklahoma can be seen. The long trail leading down the Fryingpan River valley also can be picked out.

A difficult ridge circuit could be followed for the return. To the south, the rough ridge leads to a 13,736-foot unnamed summit and on to 13,646-foot Mount Champion. From there, a return to the trailhead is down gentle slopes to a saddle east of the end of the 4WD road. However, it's best to return by the ascent route.

This hike is better to take after most of the snows are gone and the weather is dry, since the entire valley tends to be wet underfoot in the early summer.

On the trail up North Fork Lake Creek toward Deer Mountain. ➤

The tumbling waters of North Fork Lake Creek, on the way to Deer Mountain.

Deer Mountain in the distance, as seen from the Independence Pass road. Mount Champion is in the foreground along the ridge to the right.

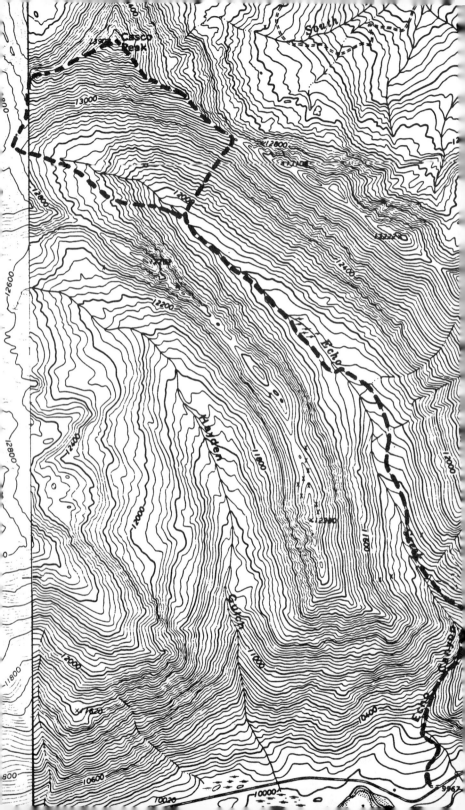

19. CASCO PEAK

Distance: 9 miles (keyhole loop)
Starting elevation: 9,970 feet
High point: 13,908 feet
Elevation gain: 4,000 feet
Rating: difficult
Time allowed: 10 hours
Maps: 7.5 minute Mount Elbert
    7.5 minute Independence Pass (extreme edge only)
    San Isabel National Forest

This strenuous hike is to Casco Peak, one of Colorado's hundred highest summits. The beginning of the hike takes you up a beautiful canyon and past some old mine relics. Then it's a stiff climb to a ridge and a scenic ridge walk to the summit. In the valley below lie the bare-boned remains of a downed aircraft. This may not be the easiest route to Casco Peak, but it's certainly the most interesting.

The trailhead is on Colorado 82, between US 24 and Independence Pass. From the east, go twelve and one-half miles west of US 24. Or, from the west, go eleven and one-half miles east of Independence Pass. Look for a gravel road on the north side of the highway about a mile west of Monitor Rock.

Some new private homes in the area may make finding the proper road difficult. As the highway swings to the west-southwest just west of Echo Creek, the correct road to take goes directly west. Leave the highway and immediately find a suitable parking place on the left side of this road.

In this area, you are on private property, but at this writing the present owner permits parking and access to Echo Canyon for hikers. Once to a parking place just off the highway, walk directly north on an old road leading up the hill. To respect the private property restrictions, do not attempt to drive up this road.

In less than a half mile, the road reaches a creek crossing at the site of a concrete building foundation. After less than a quarter of a mile farther, the road is washed out. Here, it's best to find a trail on the east side of Echo Canyon, which climbs steeply at times for another half mile.

This half mile brings you to an intersection where a dim trail follows the creek to the left and an old road bears sharply to the right. Follow the road, which soon switches back to the northwest and continues on the north side of Echo Creek. Continue northwest for another half mile to an intersection where another road takes off up the hill to the right. Keep on the path straight ahead.

As you continue up the canyon, the trail on the old road gets increasingly worse and finally runs out in thick willows. Head uphill to the right and skirt the willows on one of several game trails.

As you go farther up the canyon, Casco Peak stands out to the northwest. At about 11,900 feet, where the canyon is comparatively level, head uphill to the north toward the first low saddle southeast of Casco Peak. Pick the easiest route up the steep hillside for a climb of about a thousand feet to the saddle at 12,860 feet. From the saddle, it's another thousand-foot climb along the ridge to the northwest in a distance of 0.7 miles. Stay generally on the top of the ridge for the easiest ascent on this final climb.

Both on the final ridge climb and from the peak, you can look down to the northeast into South Half Moon Creek valley. To the north and slightly east of Casco Peak is another of Colorado's highest hundred peaks, 13,940-foot French Mountain. Another peak—an unnamed 13,823er to the southwest only two miles away—can be seen from the Casco Peak summit. The Fourteeners —Massive, Elbert, and La Plata—dominate the view to the north, east, and south, respectively.

On the way up, perhaps you didn't notice the remains of the downed aircraft in the upper reaches of Echo Creek valley. If you can spot these remains from Casco Peak, you can follow a route toward them as you descend through the basin. The best way is to descend the ridge leading west-southwest from Casco Peak. Continue down this ridge to a saddle at 12,940 feet. Then drop down to the east into the head of Echo Creek basin.

From the aircraft, continue down, following Echo Creek until you pick up the trail in the creek valley. In wet periods, portions of the Echo Creek basin may be swampy and muddy underfoot.

Old ore crusher along the trail to Casco Peak.

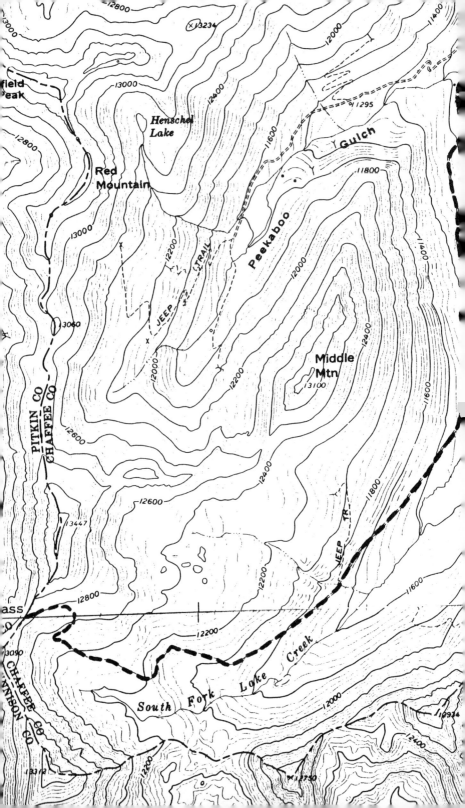

20. RED MOUNTAIN PASS

Distance: 7 miles (out and back)
Starting elevation: 10,940 feet
High point: 12,860 feet
Elevation gain: 1,950 feet
Rating: easy
Time allowed: 4 to 5 hours
Maps: 7.5 minute Independence Pass
   7.5 minute Pieplant
   San Isabel National Forest

This is an interesting hike to a scenic Continental Divide pass, and it follows an old road all the way. The road to the trailhead is rough and steep in spots, but under good conditions most cars can make it. This pass is not named on either the USGS topographic maps or the national forest maps. It is located right at the border of the Independence Pass and Pieplant topographic maps.

Drive on Colorado 82 for fourteen and one-half miles west of US 24, or east from Aspen nine and one-half miles beyond Independence Pass to the South Fork road. Take this unpaved road south across the creek. At 2.5 miles, a side road goes left to Sayres Gulch, and at 3.3 miles, another side road goes uphill on the right to McNasser Gulch. Continue past these road intersections to a road fork in a broad valley for a total of four and one-half miles. Park near the old building just beyond the road fork.

Walk up the left fork of the road, which soon turns into 4WD quality. After walking about one and one-half miles, notice the pass across the creek to the left. This flat pass is Lake Pass, which once had a wagon road on its north side. Little or no trace of the road remains on the gravel-strewn side of the ridge, but it is interesting to guess where the route might have been.

Continue on the 4WD road, circling to the west at the base of Middle Mountain. Soon there are some rock slides that effectively stop vehicle traffic. However, the route of the old road is evident as it continues on the south slopes, past old mines, to the pass. The ridge point almost two miles to the north is named "Red Mountain" on maps, but the entire ridge is a distinctive red color.

The road over the pass once continued down the west side to mines and to Ruby, now a ghost town. However, much of this road has now disappeared, so admire the view and return the way you came.

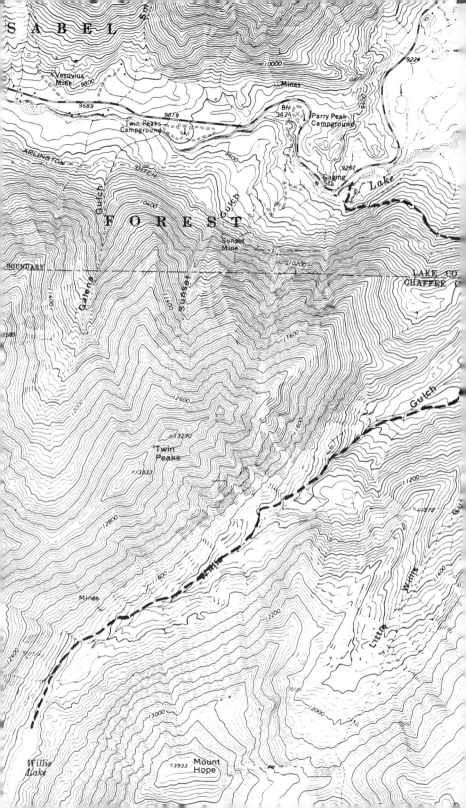

21. WILLIS LAKE

Distance: 11 miles (out and back)
Starting elevation: 9,280 feet
High point: 11,760 feet
Elevation gain: 2,400 feet
Rating: moderate
Time allowed: 8 or 9 hours
Maps: 7.5 minute Mount Elbert
San Isabel National Forest

Willis Lake is a large, high lake set in a beautiful cirque. It is usually said to have good fishing. However, the lake is too far from the trailhead to allow much fishing time except for backpackers. It makes an excellent day hike.

The trailhead is near the paved highway west of Twin Lakes Reservoir. From US 24, drive eight and a half miles west on Colorado 82 to a point almost two miles west of the village of Twin Lakes. From Aspen, you can reach the same spot by following Colorado 82 eastward fifteen and a half miles beyond Independence Pass to a point just over a half mile east of Parry Peak Campground. Turn southwest on a narrow gravel road that parallels the highway and leads a hundred yards to a trailhead parking and camping area on the north side of Lake Creek.

Hike south across Lake Creek on a substantial bridge. Turn right and walk southwest a hundred yards along an old road. Look for a trail on the left (south) side of the road.

Walk up the trail, which may be hard to locate because of heavy underbrush, and across a swampy area as the trail bears to the east. Continue on the trail about a half mile to a junction. Take the right fork up the hill, and proceed up several steep sections. After a mile, the trail joins another trail along the Arlington Ditch. The Arlington Ditch once carried water from Lake Creek several miles west of the trailhead to points eastward. The abandoned ditch with the trail alongside gives you a half mile of level walking.

Follow the trail eastward until it brings you to Willis Gulch, which is the outlet from Willis Lake. Parts of Arlington Ditch and the trail itself have disappeared because of large earth slides. The route across these slides is obvious, but the hillside is steep, and walking the narrow trail requires care.

Lake Creek as it winds between huge boulders near the start of the trail to Willis Lake.

In the early summer, Willis Gulch carries a torrent of water down its steep channel. If the water is too high to safely cross when you first reach Willis Gulch, continue upstream about fifty yards on a faint trail to a solid log crossing with a handrail.

Cross Willis Gulch to the wide trail on the east side. Turn right on this trail, which was once an old road. Be sure to carefully note the place where you reached the trail on the east side of Willis Gulch so that you won't miss it on the way back.

Hike up the old road until it forks, after about a half mile. Take the right fork at this junction. The left fork follows Little Willis Gulch to a pass between Mount Hope and Quail Mountain and continues on down into the Clear Creek valley (see hike number 22). The right fork will take you to Willis Lake.

Care is required where landslides have covered portions of the trail to Willis Lake.

Mount Hope (13,933 feet) is on the left as you continue up Willis Gulch toward Willis Lake. The basin surrounding Willis Lake is circled by Mount Hope, unnamed peaks of 13,531 and 13,616 feet, and by 13,783-foot Rinker Peak, reading clockwise. Impressive north-facing cliffs on the first three of these peaks hold large snowbanks into the late summer.

As you come into sight of Willis Lake, the trail climbs the hillside to the west of the lake. If the lake is your destination, leave the trail to go directly toward it. You may want to visit the mine at the end of the trail beyond Willis Lake. The mine is easily visible as you approach the lake. If you do this, stay on the trail.

Return the same way, being careful to find the crossing of Willis Gulch to the trail along Arlington Ditch.

89

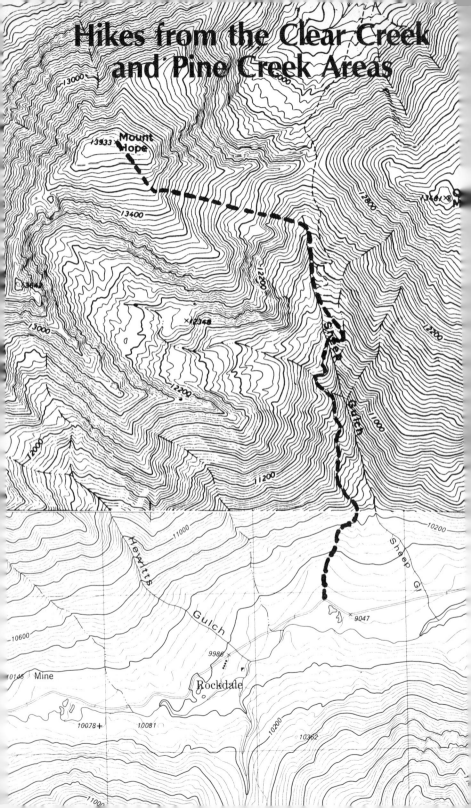

Hikes from the Clear Creek and Pine Creek Areas

22. MOUNT HOPE

Distance: 5 miles (out and back)
Starting elevation: 9,850 feet
High point: 13,933 feet
Elevation gain: 4,100 feet
Rating: moderate, short, but large elevation gain
Time allowed: 7 hours
Maps: 7.5 minute Winfield
7.5 minute Mount Elbert
San Isabel National Forest

This hike takes you up a steep scenic trail, then gives some open hiking on steep slopes to a high peak with a broad summit. The hike is better in the late summer when most of the snows are gone.

The trailhead is off the Clear Creek road, which leads west from US 24 about fifteen miles north of Buena Vista and nineteen miles south of Leadville. Drive this well-graded road eight miles to Vicksburg and then about one and one-half miles to a point where the road makes a semicircular bend to the north. Here, find a narrow road leading north. The road ends after about two hundred yards but provides some parking space.

A good trail takes off to the left near the end of the road. It follows the west side of Sheep Gulch and climbs steeply through the forest. After one and one-half miles, at about 11,300 feet, the trail enters a more open area and crosses to the east side of Sheep Gulch. It passes an old cabin as it first crosses to the east side of the gulch, then climbs up along the east side of the gulch.

The shortest route to Mount Hope leaves the trail about a half mile beyond the cabin, as the trail starts to climb the hillside east of the gulch. Continue to follow the gulch beyond the last timber, and after rounding the last cliffs on the left, bear upward to the west into a large basin. Pick out the best route to ascend in this basin. When there is a large snowfield in the upper part of the basin, it may be best to skirt it on the left. Beyond this point, at about 13,600 feet, you'll be on the southeast ridge, and the slope becomes more gentle.

As an alternate, you can get in a little more trail walking at the expense of a little rougher climb. For this approach, keep on the

Looking south up the Clohesy Lake valley from the slopes of Mount Hope. (photo by Bill Bueler)

Mountain panorama looking south from the summit of Mount Hope. (photo by Bill Bueler)

The large, flat summit of Mount Hope, with La Plata Peak in the background. (photo by Bill Bueler)

trail to the 12,540-foot pass between Mount Hope and Quail Mountain. From the pass, there's a good view to the north down Little Willis Gulch. Continue from the pass up the ridge to the west. Some of the rougher sections can be bypassed on the left.

From the summit of Mount Hope, there's a good view of La Plata Peak to the west. You'll need to walk to the west end of the summit area to get a good view down into Willis Gulch and see large Willis Lake, which is surrounded by an impressive ridge and several unnamed summits (see hike number 21).

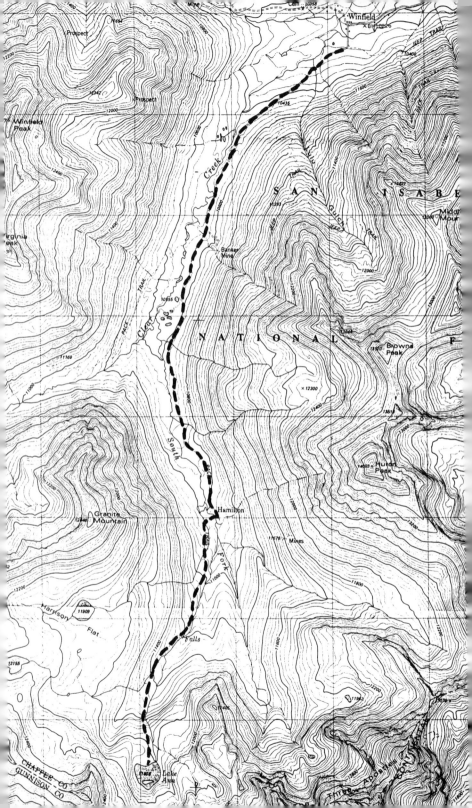

23. LAKE ANN

Distance: 13 miles (out and back)
Starting elevation: 10,250 feet
High point: 11,805 feet
Elevation gain: 1,600 feet
Rating: easy, but long, with some route finding
  involved
Time allowed: 7 to 8 hours
Maps: 7.5 minute Winfield
    San Isabel National Forest

Lake Ann is set in a stark cirque just north of the Continental Divide. Starting with a walk up a 4WD road, you continue on an interesting trail through the forest. Then you emerge in a vast open area just west of the Three Apostles for the final approach to Lake Ann. However, the latter part of the hike uses unmaintained trails that may be difficult to follow.

The trailhead is just beyond Winfield on the Clear Creek road. On US 24, drive fifteen miles north from Buena Vista, nineteen miles south from Leadville, or four miles south of the Colorado 82 and US 24 intersection, to the Clear Creek road. Follow this good but sometimes rough gravel road twelve miles west to the partially restored ghost town of Winfield.

At a "T" intersection in Winfield, turn south and cross Clear Creek on a bridge. Shortly beyond this creek crossing you'll find a large parking area on the right-hand side of the road. This is the stopping point for most regular cars. A few cars and 4WDs can go all or part of an additional two miles to a point where the road is closed.

From your parking place, walk up the 4WD road. At 0.7 miles, keep to the right, where there's another 4WD road leading left up the hill. The left fork leading uphill is the route to Browns Peak, described in hike number 24. At 1.5 miles, you will pass the large Banker Mine on the left. At the intersection of the road leading to the Banker Mine, there is also a road leading to the right toward Clear Creek, where a barrier halts vehicle traffic just before the creek crossing.

The Three Apostles as seen from the trail to Lake Ann.

Continue straight ahead for another half mile, where a barrier stops vehicle traffic. Walk along the former road beyond the barrier, crossing numerous drainages coming in from the left. Soon a dramatic view of the Three Apostles may be seen directly ahead.

After a little over a mile of walking beyond the barrier, begin looking for a trail leading off to the right. At this obscure junction, the Three Apostles are in plain view. There are several abandoned cabins across the creek to the right and a flat, open meadow ahead. The trail to the right leads to a campsite on a small knoll.

Just beyond this knoll is a trail leading downward to a creek crossing. Hopefully, there will still be a bridge of sorts made from logs lashed together. This is the best place for crossing the South Fork of Clear Creek, which must be crossed to get to Lake Ann. If you miss this crossing, other possible crossings may be found further south to gain the trail on the west side of the creek.

After crossing the creek, continue south and southwest on a not-so-well-maintained trail with frequent downed timber. After a mile or so, the trail deteriorates further. At this point, the route stays to the west of a stream and soon crosses a side stream coming in from the west. The route continues directly south, with a few paths and obscure trails to help. You enter a large flat area out of the timber as you make the final approach to Lake Ann.

The setting of Lake Ann is striking within the steep-sided cirque below the Continental Divide. To the east along the Continental Divide is the peak called West Apostle, and on the ridge further east is Ice Mountain, the highest of the Three Apostles. Ice Mountain is one of the harder climbs in the Sawatch Range.

If you found the trails on the way to Lake Ann, go back the same way. Otherwise, perhaps you can find more trail to use on the return trip.

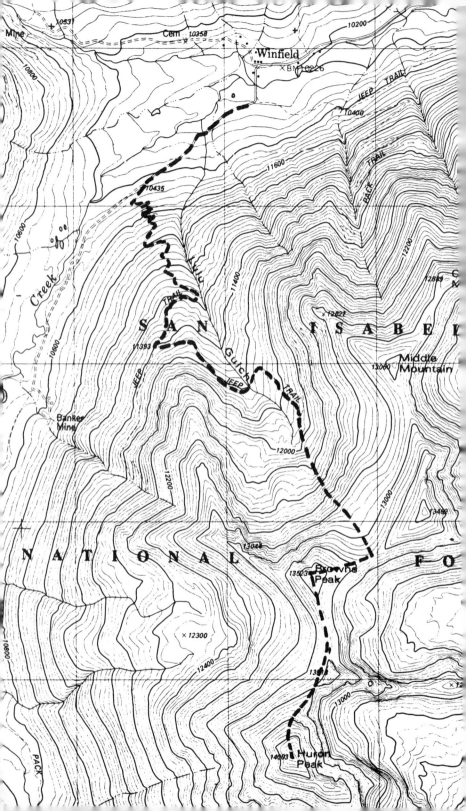

24. BROWNS PEAK AND HURON PEAK

Distance: 10 miles (out and back)
Starting elevation: 10,250 feet
High point: 14,003 feet
Elevation gain: 4,200 feet
Rating: moderate, but lots of elevation gain
Time allowed: 8 hours
Maps: 7.5 minute Winfield
        San Isabel National Forest

The traditional route up Huron Peak is a long grind, because you must climb tiresome chiprock for over 2,000 feet. The approach for that traditional route is from the southwest after a hike-in to a mine just east of Hamilton. At 14,003 feet, Huron Peak barely makes the list of Colorado's Fourteeners.

The route suggested here gives a lot more variety, with a hike up an old mine road to the flank of Browns Peak. Then there's the opportunity to climb another named summit, Browns Peak, and traverse the ridge to Huron Peak without losing a lot of elevation between the two peaks.

The trailhead is the same as for the Lake Ann hike, number 23, so refer to that hike description for directions to reach the parking area just south of Winfield.

From this parking place, walk up the 4WD road to the junction at 0.7 miles. For the hike to Browns Peak and Huron Peak, take the left fork of the 4WD road that leads up the hill. Continue on this 4WD road as it switches back and forth on the west side of a drainage. At about 11,400 feet, you'll reach a junction. Take the left fork here, as the right one soon reaches a dead end. Under good conditions, it would be possible to reach this area with a 4WD vehicle.

The road soon enters a timbered area and crosses Lulu Gulch, the drainage to the east. Then it climbs to the east to a bit over 11,900 feet before turning sharply to the north. Through this area, the road deteriorates and becomes impassable even for 4WD vehicles. Where the road turns sharply to the north, or shortly before, leave the road by turning right, and head south-southeast up the valley. From this area you can look with awe at the 4WD road zigzagging up the steep mountainside to the north.

Your objective here is to reach the saddle between Browns Peak, directly south, and the unnamed 13,462-foot summit to the southeast. The saddle, at 13,140 feet, is about three-fourths of a mile away. This climb of 1,200 feet is not difficult, though there is a steeper stretch about midway. After reaching the saddle, turn right for a short ridge walk to the summit of 13,523-foot Browns Peak.

While it is a named high point, Browns Peak is not nearly a separate summit by the definition that a separate mountain must rise at least 300 feet above saddles between it and higher points. The low point on the ridge between Browns Peak and Huron Peak is a little less than 200 feet below the summit of Browns Peak. The best route from Browns Peak to Huron is along the crest of the ridge. You can bypass a couple of ridge points on the west. It's a rocky climb to Huron Peak but only about 650 feet up from the saddle.

From the summit of Huron Peak, there's a good view directly south to the Three Apostles. Ice Mountain, an almost-Fourteener, stands out as the centerpiece. A look to the east shows Missouri Mountain, only a few feet higher than Huron Peak, with Iowa and Emerald Peaks on the ridge running south.

For the return trip, it would be possible to bypass the summit of Browns Peak, but with the small amount of climbing involved, it's probably easier to go back over the summit. Follow the rest of the route the way you came.

Carefully following a snow-covered trail.

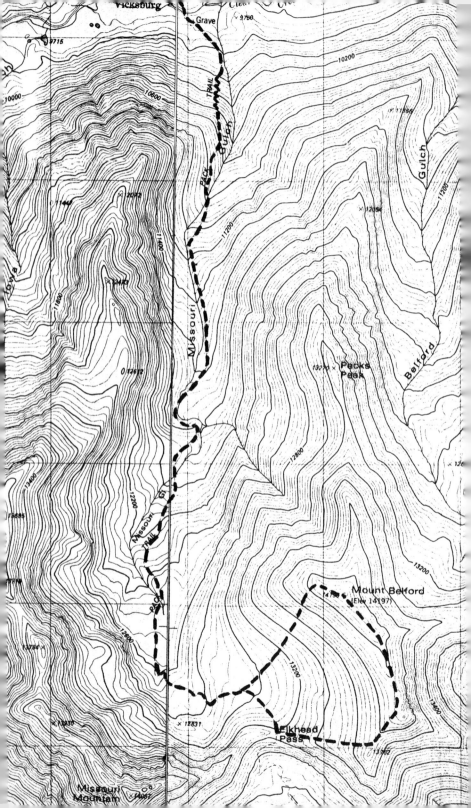

25. ELKHEAD PASS AND MOUNT BELFORD

Distance: 12 miles (keyhole loop)
Starting elevation: 9,660 feet
High point: 14,197 feet
Elevation gain: 4,600 feet
Rating: easy walking, but long and with lots of
* elevation gain*
Time allowed: 9 or 10 hours
Maps: 7.5 minute Winfield
*   7.5 minute Mount Harvard*
*   San Isabel National Forest*

Many people take hikes just to climb 14,000-foot peaks. This is a hike on a trail to one of the highest passes in Colorado. It takes you so near the top of 14,197-foot Mount Belford that you'll probably want to walk to the summit just "because it's there."

The trailhead is at Vicksburg on the Clear Creek road. On US 24, go fifteen miles north of Buena Vista, or nineteen miles south of Leadville, and turn west for eight miles on a gravel road to Vicksburg.

From a large parking area on the south side of the road, walk up the well-constructed trail as it starts gaining altitude rapidly with many switchbacks. The grade decreases as the trail enters the valley and passes through an area usually having overgrown brush. Rain pants may be desirable to wear if the brush is wet. Higher in the valley, the trail sometimes is harder to follow, but the route is obvious as it winds up the drainage to the south.

Elkhead Pass, at 13,220 feet, is the low point on the ridge between Mount Belford to the east and 14,067-foot Missouri Mountain to the west. It may be a low point here, but it is one of the highest named passes in Colorado. The dominant mountain looking south from the pass is 14,420-foot Mount Harvard. You also can look down from the pass into Pine Creek valley. With suitable transportation arrangements, you could follow the trail over Elkhead Pass to join the Pine Creek trail and after ten more miles emerge at the Pine Creek trailhead for hike number 26.

Bridge over Clear Creek at the start of the trail to Elkhead Pass.

From Elkhead Pass, the gentle route up the ridge east and then north to the summit of Mount Belford can readily be seen. This is in contrast to the jagged ridge leading west to Missouri Mountain. The climb to Mount Belford involves an additional mile and 900 feet of elevation gain.

To the east, separated from Mount Belford by a dip of 650 feet, is 14,153-foot Mount Oxford. Save the Mount Oxford climb for the more interesting approach described in hike number 26.

To return from Mount Belford, you need not go back to Elkhead Pass, since you can find an easy descent to the northwest and west to reach the trail in the valley north of the pass. Another possibility is to follow the ridge and steeper slopes to the north to reach the trail nearer the trailhead. This is the so-called "normal" route for climbing Mount Belford, shorter and steeper, but less interesting than the one by way of Elkhead Pass. So we suggest descending to the northwest and following the trail back to the trailhead.

The ridge up Mount Belford from Elkhead Pass. (photo by Art Tauchen)

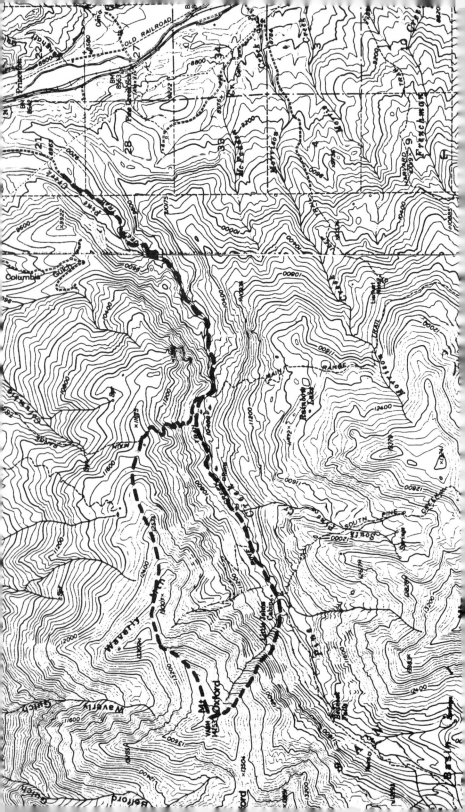

26. PINE CREEK TRAIL AND MOUNT OXFORD

Distance: 16 miles (keyhole loop)
Starting elevation: 8,920 feet
High point: 14,153 feet
Elevation gain: 5,400 feet
Rating: difficult
Time allowed: 10 to 12 hours
Maps: 7.5 minute Harvard Lakes
7.5 minute Mount Harvard
San Isabel National Forest

Most guidebooks suggest climbing Mount Oxford as an afterthought to climbing Mount Belford, approaching from Vicksburg to the north. In this hike, Mount Oxford is the primary objective. The approach is from the east. It's a more scenic and interesting climb but certainly a bit longer and somewhat harder.

The trailhead is on the Pine Creek road. On US 24, thirteen miles north of Buena Vista, or twenty-one miles south of Leadville, turn west on a gravel road, Chaffee County 388. At 0.3 miles, continue straight ahead where the more prominent road turns right. At 0.6 miles, the road makes a sharp turn up the hill to the right. The stopping place for many regular cars is before this turn, so we'll consider that area to be the trailhead.

With 4WD, and under good conditions with some regular cars, take the right turn up the hill and continue for another mile to an informal camping area. Regular cars should park at the camping area, but 4WDs may continue, taking the left-hand road to skirt the camping area on the south. After a mile, there's a choice of routes, and the left fork is the better. After a quarter mile, the 4WD road ends. An excellent trail begins here. A locked gate may prevent driving the 4WD section.

Whether you've reached this point by hiking or by vehicle, continue on the trail, crossing the Main Range Trail after two more miles. Another two miles brings you to Harry Littlejohn's cabin (shown on some maps as "Little Johns Cabin") at 10,700 feet.

The rushing waters of Pine Creek in the early summer.

Mount Belford as seen from Mount Oxford. (photo by Art Tauchen) ➤

Now the climb begins. Go just west of the stream coming from the north. Head northwest through the timber, staying on the ridge west of the watercourse. Aspen groves, large boulders, and other assorted hindrances will impede your progress. The next mile and a half involve an elevation gain of 2,350 feet. The first portion is the hardest. Above timberline, the going is easier. When you can't go up any farther, you'll be at the top of Mount Oxford.

To the west a mile, and with 650-foot drop to the saddle plus another climb of 700 feet, is Mount Belford. You may want to leave that for another day, when you try hike number 25.

For a variation on the return, descend on the ridge to the east-northeast. Staying on top of this ridge brings you to a saddle southwest of the higher northwestern summit of Waverly Mountain. If you want to climb the true summit of Waverly Mountain, it's an easy walk to the 13,292-foot point less than a quarter mile ahead.

If you've climbed the higher summit of Waverly Mountain, descend to the southeast to the saddle between it and the lower 13,007-foot summit. If you didn't choose to climb the higher summit, contour on its south flanks to the saddle between the summits.

Contour north of the lower summit to regain the crest of the ridge leading east. Continue east along this ridge. After you reach the forest, it will be about a half mile through fairly open timber to get to the good-quality Main Range Trail.

Go to the right on the Main Range Trail, and follow it south for one and one-half miles to the junction with the Pine Creek Trail. From here, it's four miles east on the Pine Creek Trail and 4WD road back to the trailhead.

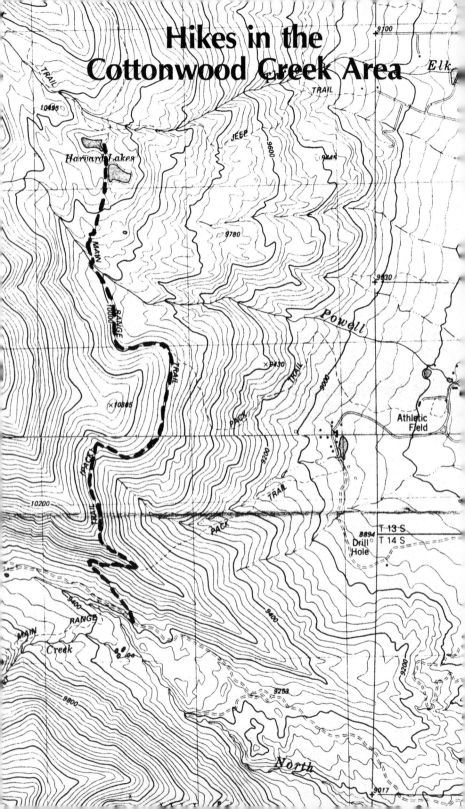

Hikes in the
Cottonwood Creek Area

27. HARVARD LAKES

Distance: 6 miles (out and back)
Starting elevation: 9,420 feet
High point: 10,280 feet
Elevation gain: 1,050 feet
Rating: easy
Time allowed: 4 hours
Maps: 7.5 minute Buena Vista West
7.5 minute Harvard Lakes
San Isabel National Forest

This is a pleasant hike along a good trail to two scenic lakes. The walk follows the Main Range Trail, which extends along the eastern side of the Sawatch Range.

The trailhead is on the North Cottonwood Creek road. From the intersection of US 24 and County 306 in Buena Vista, go north a half mile, and turn west on Crossman Avenue. Two miles west at a "T," turn right and go north and northwest a mile on a county road. Where the road turns north, make a sharp turn south over a cattle guard, and follow the gravel road, Chaffee County 365, south a quarter mile, and then west. Three and half miles on this rough road bring you to the Main Range Trail. There's a bit of parking space on the south side of the road, just east of the trailhead, which is on the north side.

While there isn't a lot of elevation to be gained on this hike, more than half of it comes within the first three-fourths of a mile. So you can slowly follow the long switchbacks as the first section of the trail leads around a ridge before it levels off at about 10,000 feet. The trail winds along at about that elevation, with one descent of about 100 feet, for nearly two miles. In this section, it alternately crosses ravines in the deep forest and winds around exposed sections of a ridge, giving good views of the valley below. After that, it climbs up a more rocky section before reaching the lakes.

While this trail is at a relatively low elevation, it is partly in the heavy forest, which sometimes retains snowbanks well into the summer.

The first of the Harvard Lakes that you'll reach can be seen off to the right of the trail and a bit lower. Then a couple of hundred yards farther is the second lake, to the left of the trail. The Harvard

Lakes are good fishing spots, so you may find fishermen in the area.

If you want to go another hundred yards on the trail, there's a junction with the trail up Three Elk Creek where it crosses the Main Range Trail. There would be many more miles of scenic walking if you wanted to continue north on the Main Range Trail.

However, this is a hike to Harvard Lakes, so the return is back over the same route.

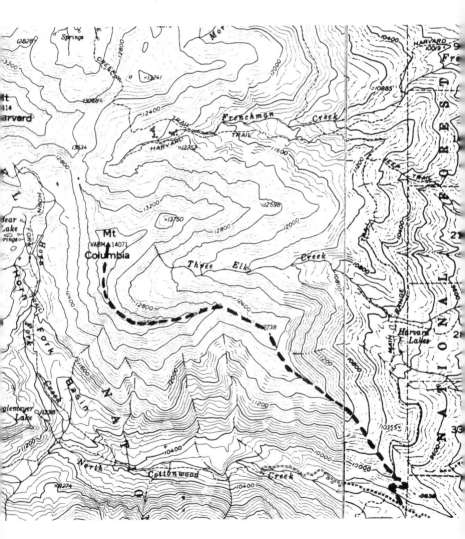

28. MOUNT COLUMBIA
VIA THE SOUTHEAST RIDGE

Distance: 10 miles (out and back)
Starting elevation: 9,420 feet
High point: 14,073 feet
Elevation gain: 4,900 feet
Rating: difficult because of the large elevation gain
Time allowed: 10 to 12 hours
Maps: 7.5 minute Buena Vista West
      7.5 minute Harvard Lakes
      7.5 minute Mount Harvard
      San Isabel National Forest

Many trail guides assume that you only want to climb Mount Columbia as an afterthought when climbing Mount Harvard. This accords Mount Columbia only secondary status as one of the Collegiate Peaks after the higher Mount Harvard, Mount Princeton, and Mount Yale. However, Mount Columbia is too fine a mountain for such treatment. It's more interesting to climb it on a separate hike. One of the most challenging routes is to follow the southeast ridge all the way to the top. Admittedly, it is longer and has more elevation gain than other approaches that can be found on Columbia alone. However, once you've followed it, you'll have seen an entirely different part of Mount Columbia and will have gained the satisfaction of reaching it by a challenging route.

This hike starts out just like the one to Harvard Lakes (number 27), but you'd better have a lot more energy in reserve for this one. Refer to the Harvard Lakes hike for directions to the trailhead. Follow the first steep switchbacks on the Main Range Trail to where the trail levels out and turns north at 10,000 feet. At this point, leave the trail to the left, and head northwest up the wooded ridge. The route is relatively open through the forest, and it's best to stay near the top of the ridge. The woodsy ridge gives you 1,200 feet of climbing in about a mile before reaching open country. A mile of scenic ridge walking as the ridge turns somewhat northward leads to a false summit at 12,740 feet.

After climbing this false summit, you get to a more level area, then come to a steeper slope. You finally reach another mostly level stretch with a few ups and downs. The walking is not difficult through these sections, as there are alternately sections of tundra and rocks. A little higher than 13,500 feet, follow the rocky ridge as it swings toward the north and leads directly to the summit.

From the top of Mount Columbia, the most striking view is toward Mount Harvard to the northwest. The ragged ridge between the two Fourteeners shows why most climbers traversing the two peaks choose to drop down to the flats on the east side rather than follow the ridge route. The ridge to Mount Harvard gives quite a contrast to the southeast ridge of Mount Columbia that you've just followed to reach the summit.

Other possible routes up Mount Columbia can be picked out. One is the short but steep scree slope from Horn Fork Basin to the west. Another is the ridge leading directly south to the trail along North Cottonwood Creek. The east ridge and the trail along Frenchman Creek are other approach routes that are used.

For the return, if you have transportation waiting at the end of the North Cottonwood Creek road, we might suggest a slide down the scree into Horn Fork Basin. Otherwise, you should look at the sights to the east as you return along the southeast ridge.

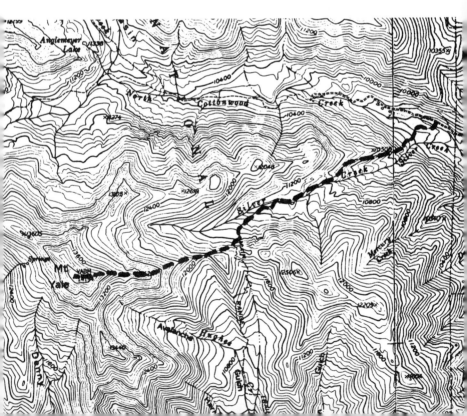

29. MOUNT YALE VIA EAST RIDGE

Distance: 12 miles (out and back)
Starting elevation: 9,420 feet
High point: 14,196 feet
Elevation gain: 4,900 feet
Rating: difficult, because it's long with lots of elevation
  gain
Time allowed: 10 hours
Maps: 7.5 minute Mount Yale
    7.5 minute Buena Vista West
    San Isabel National Forest

Mount Yale makes one of the best peak climbs in the Sawatch Range. Perhaps one reason is the diversity of interesting routes, which permits approaches from several directions. The shortest and quickest are from the Cottonwood Pass road to the south, so most guide books emphasize those routes. However, perhaps the most scenic and interesting route approaches from the northeast, and that's the one described here. This route also permits you to go higher on good-quality trail than the shorter southern routes.

The trailhead is on the North Cottonwood Creek road. From the intersection of US 24 and County 306 in Buena Vista, go north a half mile, and turn west on Crossman Avenue. Two miles west at a "T," turn right and go north and northwest a mile on county road. Where the road turns north, make a sharp turn south over a cattle guard, and follow the gravel road, Chaffee County 365, south a quarter mile, and then west. Three and a half miles on this rough road brings you to the Main Range Trail. First you reach the portion leading north, and a quarter mile further is our trailhead. There's parking at a small clearing here.

Under good conditions, the road to the trailhead is passable by passenger cars, although some may prefer to stop a mile or two short of the trailhead at some rough steep sections. Hike up the Main Range Trail to the south. The trail is excellent but steepens after a mile as it climbs along Silver Creek.

After reaching about 10,800 feet, the grade slackens, and the trail breaks out into a scenic open area from which the summit of

Mount Yale viewed from a large meadow along the Main Range Trail.

Mount Yale can be seen ahead. After crossing this open area, which offers good camping spots, follow the trail as it crosses Silver Creek and begins to climb toward the south. With several switchbacks, continue climbing toward the 11,900-foot pass along the east ridge of Mount Yale. Look for the last switchback where the trail turns left, to the east, below the pass. Near this switchback, climb up the slope to the right to reach the ridge west of a small ridge point. If you happen to go all the way to the pass, climb westward over that ridge point.

The route from here is directly along the ridge toward the west. The ridge is an interesting climb with its succession of rock piles interspersed with flat tundra areas. Generally, it's best to go over the top of each rock pile, unless an obviously easier way can be seen around the side. About halfway along the two-mile ridge, after you pass a 13,420-foot ridge point, the grade becomes noticeably less steep. On the final stretch to the summit, you may see other hikers approaching the peak from the south.

The climbing route along the east ridge of Mount Yale, from the point on the ridge just after leaving the trail.

Return by the same route, or if you want to try a little route finding, there are two alternates that can be used. One is to return on the ridge about a half mile until the slopes to the north offer an easy descent. Come down from the ridge on the rocky slopes, then turn east down the valley. Stay on the north side of Silver Creek as you enter the forest, and follow along the north side of the creek until you meet the trail.

Another return possibility involves more ridge walking, with perhaps an additional 500 feet of climbing. For this route, head northwest off the summit for about a quarter of a mile, until you can turn northeast along another connecting ridge. Continue to follow this northeast ridge as it curves to the east. There'll be climbs over five separate ridge points, but the walking generally is very good—much easier than the rocky parts of the east ridge. After reaching the last ridge point at 11,625 feet, come off the ridge to the south through a clearing area. A short stretch through the timber will bring you back to the trail on the north side of Silver Creek.

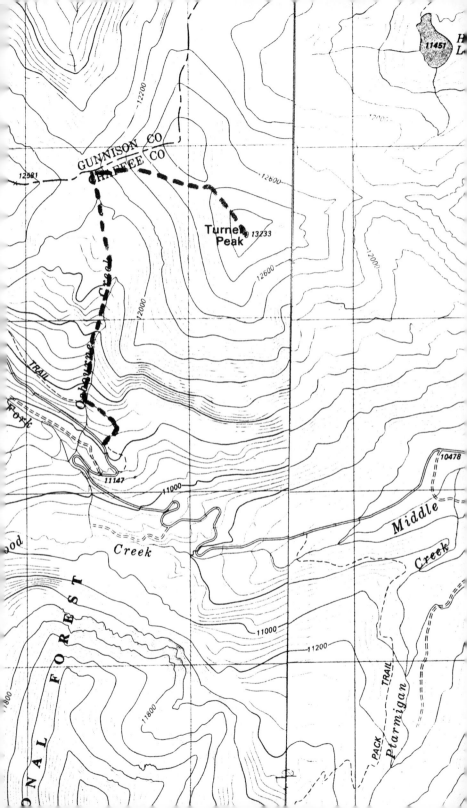

30. OSBOURNE CREEK
   AND TURNER PEAK

Distance: 5 miles (out and back)
Starting elevation: 11,220
High point: 13,233 feet
Elevation gain: 2,100 feet
Rating: moderate, but short
Time allowed: 4 to 5 hours
Maps: 7.5 minute Tincup
      San Isabel National Forest

This short hike takes you through a scenic valley to an unnamed Continental Divide pass, then up a steep hillside to a newly named but seldom climbed peak, which is the high point in the general area.

The starting point is on County 306, between Buena Vista and Cottonwood Pass. Drive west from Buena Vista about seventeen miles, toward Cottonwood Pass. From Taylor Park, drive three miles east of Cottonwood Pass.

The hike starts near a point where the road completes a switchback, with both arms turning back toward the west. Two hundred yards west up the road from this switchback, there is a wide graded gravel area north of the road. You can park in this area or on a spur road leading west from the switchback.

Hike north out of the graded area to an old roadbed paralleling the main road. Follow the roadbed north up the hill and then northwest into a level area. In this stretch, you're following the route of the original Cottonwood Pass road. The level area once was the site of a halfway station on the stagecoach route.
Cottonwood Pass road. If you look carefully,. you can see the remains of the old halfway station on the stagecoach route.

Beyond this area is the crossing of Osbourne Creek, which may be flowing full in the early season and have little or no water after the snows are gone.

After you've walked past the site of the halfway station, cross Osbourne Creek. About fifty yards beyond the creek, look for the start of an obscure trail on the right-hand side of the road. This trail

Looking north from the Continental Divide pass above Osbourne Creek. Across the valley the Continental Divide winds its way back to the west.

is marked by old blazes on the trees, but the tread is faint and the start may be difficult to spot. In any event, head north through the open timber on the west side of Osbourne Creek. The trail is sometimes near the creek and sometimes as much as a hundred yards away, so if you didn't find the beginning, you may be able to get onto it later.

After a half mile or so, the trail runs out as the route leaves the timber. Continue north through the scattered willows toward the obvious pass ahead. The best route stays to the west of Osbourne Creek as the grade slackens, and you get superb views to the south.

Continue on to the unnamed Continental Divide pass at 12,060 feet. From this pass, a vast new panorama unfolds as you look to the north across the South Texas Creek valley. To the left are the Three Apostles, with rugged Ice Mountain as the centerpiece. To the right of the Three Apostles is Huron Peak in the distance. Then come several unnamed summits along the Continental Divide, with Emerald Peak the high point on the right.

From the pass, it's almost 1,200 feet of elevation to our objective,

Turner Peak from the Ptarmigan Lake trail.

in a little less than a mile. Start up the ridge to the east, bearing to the right of the first rocky part. As the ridge becomes less steep, you can head more to the right to bypass the ridge point directly east of the pass. Aim for the 12,780-foot saddle between that point and the higher summit to the south. From the saddle, it is a 450-foot climb to the summit.

If you're not interested in the spectacular view from the pass and only want to climb Turner Peak, you could head up its steep western side from the Osbourne Creek valley before reaching the pass.

The 13,233-foot Turner Peak is the highest point in the general area west of Mount Yale. The Turner Peak summit rises more than a thousand feet above Cottonwood Pass to the west and Browns Pass to the northeast. Turner Peak was officially named in 1976.

After admiring the views from the top, follow much the same route on the return. However, it's not necessary to go all the way back to the pass if you prefer to descend to the Osbourne Creek valley somewhat to the south of the pass.

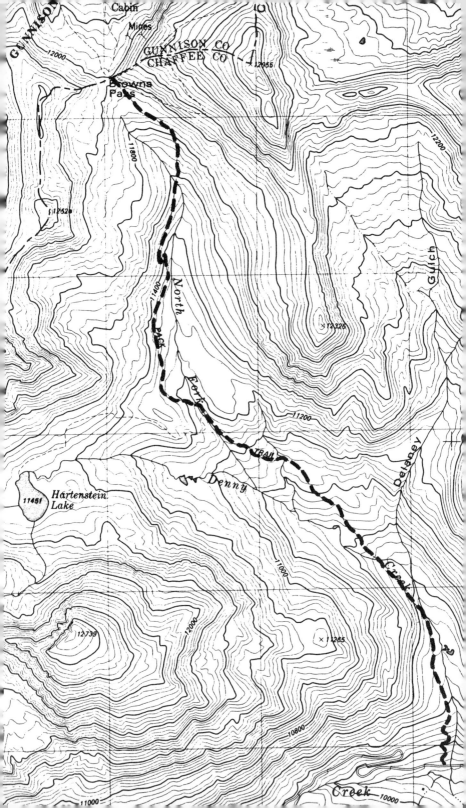

31. BROWNS PASS

Distance: 8 miles (out and back)
Starting elevation: 9,900 feet
High point: 12,020 feet
Elevation gain: 2,100 feet
Rating: easy
Time allowed: 6 hours
Maps: 7.5 minute Mount Yale
San Isabel National Forest

The hike to Browns Pass is entirely on well-established trail, is scenic, and offers outstanding views when the objective is reached.

The starting point is on County 306 between Buena Vista and Cottonwood Pass, about twelve miles west of Buena Vista. The trailhead is just west of Denny Creek, which is a half mile west of the Collegiate Peaks Campground. The newly constructed trailhead also serves as a starting point for hikes to Hartenstein Lake. Since the initial portion of the trail serves both Hartenstein Lake and Browns Pass, it is one of the most popular trails in the area. The road between Buena Vista and Cottonwood Pass has been improved in recent years, making this trailhead easy to reach. When approaching from the Taylor River country, the trailhead is about eight miles east of Cottonwood Pass.

The trail follows an old 4WD road heading north and northwest, which is now closed to vehicular traffic. Continue for about two miles on this sometimes steep 4WD road. After crossing Denny Creek, the route proceeds northwest, finally reaching a junction point in a level, open area. From this point, the 4WD road continues westward to Hartenstein Lake, while the Browns Pass route becomes a trail. This trail crosses a small bridge westward, then bears northwesterly as it leaves the 4WD road. From the trail junction, Browns Pass is almost directly northward.

For the next mile, the trail, constructed in recent years, is a good-quality graded trail, but it becomes muddy in wet weather. After a mile or so through the forest, the trail breaks out into the open as it approaches Browns Pass. During this stretch, the views to the south are most impressive.

Browns Pass is a Continental Divide pass, and the scene from the

Denny Creek near the start of the trail to Browns Pass.

Looking back at Mount Princeton on the route to Browns Pass.

top is into the Texas Creek drainage west of the Continental Divide. Strangely enough, the ridge of impressive mountains directly across the valley to the north is also along the Continental Divide. This is because the divide takes a swing to the east through Browns Pass, then makes a loop back to the west at the head of the Texas Creek valley.

Directly across the valley north of Browns Pass is an impressive unnamed 13,762-foot summit, the highest unnamed peak in this area. Farther to the west are the Three Apostles, the middle one of which is the rugged 13,951-foot Ice Mountain.

From Browns Pass, the trail continues down into the Texas Creek valley, passing Browns Cabin in less than a mile. This cabin would make a good extension of the Browns Pass hike. For many years, the cabin has been maintained in good enough condition to serve as an overnight stop for backpackers. So if you find others at this cabin, they are likely to be visitors just like yourself.

Another trail from Browns Pass heads up the ridge to the east and eventually leads to Kroenke Lake, in the North Cottonwood Creek drainage to the east. The trail continues beyond Kroenke Lake to the end of the North Cottonwood Creek road. This trail would make a good one-way trip if transportation were arranged. For this out-and-back day hike, return to the trailhead the way you came.

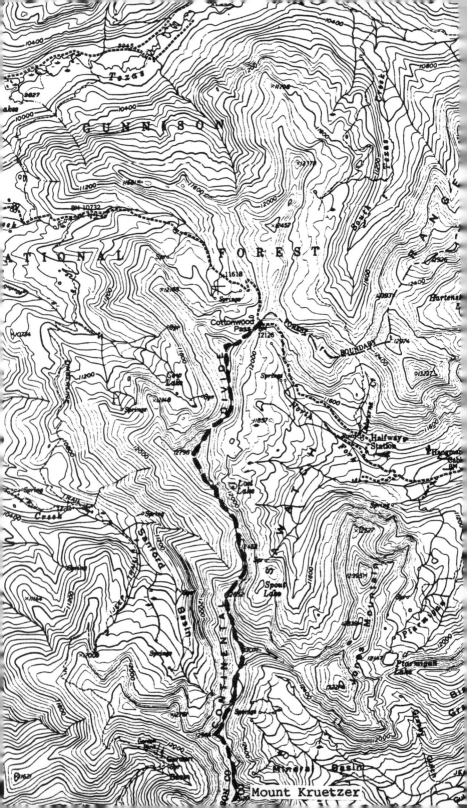

32. COTTONWOOD PASS
TO MOUNT KREUTZER

Distance: 12 miles (out and back)
Starting elevation: 12,126 feet
High point: 13,095 feet
Elevation gain: 4,750 feet
Rating: moderate, but long and all at high altitude
Time allowed: 8 hours
Maps: 7.5 minute Tincup
    San Isabel National Forest
    Gunnison National Forest

The Sawatch Range provides much interesting and not-too-difficult ridge walking. Usually the best place to start is at one of the high passes. This hike is entirely along the Continental Divide. There is no trail, but the route is open, and there are no great difficulties. The objective, Mount Kreutzer, is a 13,095-foot summit six miles south of Cottonwood Pass.

While the elevation of Mount Kreutzer is less than a thousand feet higher than Cottonwood Pass, there's a total of 4,750 feet of elevation to be gained during the round trip. You'll climb over three distinct, unnamed, separate summits, at 12,580, 12,792, and 13,055 feet, and several other ridge points. The profile on the way to Mount Kreutzer, ignoring elevation changes of less than a hundred feet, goes something like this: +454 −320 +532 −572 +630 −190 +395 −315 +240 −160 +275 feet. If you stay on the Continental Divide, there's a total climb of 2,850 feet and a net elevation gain of nearly a thousand feet. Then there are the 1,900 feet to be climbed on the return trip, making the total of 4,750 feet of elevation gain for the trip.

The starting point is Cottonwood Pass, on County 306, twenty miles west of Buena Vista and fourteen miles east of Taylor Park. Ample parking is available. The route begins with a climb of the 12,580-foot summit to the southwest. For the first mile or two, there are trails of use made by the many tourists visiting the pass, but soon the Continental Divide route becomes less traveled. Once across the 12,580-foot summit, there's a drop to a 12,260-foot pass and then

The approach to Cottonwood Pass from the east. The hike to Mount Kreutzer is along the ridge to the left.

12,260-foot pass and then a substantial climb to a 12,792-foot summit. Throughout this section, there are good views of the Cottonwood Pass road and the valleys below.

Continue along the ridge for another two miles, over several small ridge points, and finally climb to a 13,055-foot summit. This point marks the junction of the Continental Divide ridge with the ridge leading east to Jones Mountain. The high point of Jones is 13,218 feet at the south end, while there is a separate 12,995-foot summit to the north. Another mile and a half, with a few ups and downs, brings you to the final 275-foot climb of Mount Kreutzer.

From the summit, you can look east into Mineral Basin and see the mining activity on the south side of Jones Mountain. To the west is the town of Tincup. The return is back north along the Continental Divide.

Some climbing can be avoided by contouring around some of the ridge points. However, the most interesting hike is to stay on the crest of the Continental Divide. There are shorter routes to Mount Kreutzer, such as from Mineral Basin or from Tincup, but the hike from Cottonwood Pass is by far the most interesting.

Most of this hike is easy tundra walking, but there are some rocky sections that are not difficult but that require care. In the summer season, tundra wild flowers are so numerous that it is difficult to avoid stepping on them.

Because the entire hike is above 12,000 feet and is on the exposed ridge, it should only be attempted in good conditions with the intention to turn back if the weather turns bad. Being all above 12,000 feet makes the hike more strenuous than the distance and elevation gain might suggest, so be sure that you're acclimated to the elevation.

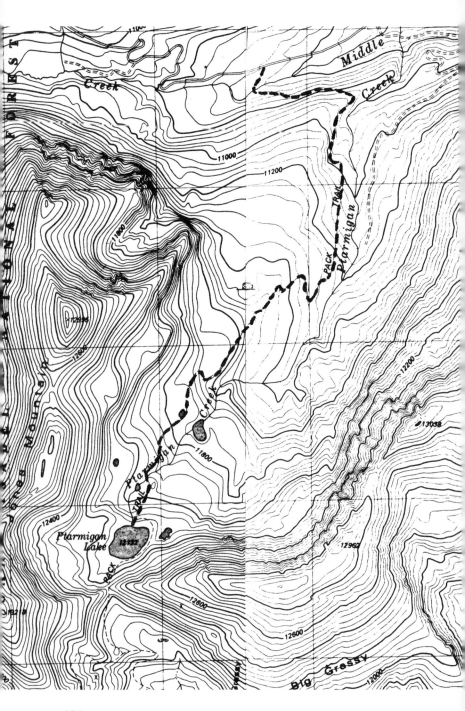

33. PTARMIGAN LAKE

Distance: 8 miles (out and back)
Starting elevation: 10,675 feet
High point: 12,132 feet
Elevation gain: 1,500 feet
Rating: easy
Time allowed: 5 to 6 hours
Maps: 7.5 minute Mount Yale
      7.5 minute Tincup
      San Isabel National Forest

Here's a chance to follow an easy trail to a scenic lake. You may have some company, because it's a popular fishing lake. The trail to Ptarmigan Lake is a good one that was built in recent years. Some say overbuilt, because sometimes you'll think you're on a boulevard rather than a trail. In any case, the trail leads to a lake set in a scenic, rocky cirque just below an unnamed pass.

The trailhead is near County 306 between Buena Vista and Cottonwood Pass. Drive west from Buena Vista about fifteen miles, or east five miles from Cottonwood Pass. Turn south on a spur road that leads a hundred yards to a parking area. Hike south on the trail from the parking area, descending to the creek. The trail crosses Middle Cottonwood Creek on a good bridge. It immediately swings to the east, where it traverses on the north side of a steep hill. The trail narrows in spots, especially as it crosses a large rock slide. After rounding a ridge, the trail swings to the south through the forest.

You can't get lost following this trail, as you notice the large number of trees that were removed to build such a wide trail. Perhaps it is for horses, two abreast. For about three miles, the trail climbs through the forest, finally reaching an open area and a small lakelet.

The trail becomes less steep as it continues up the basin below Ptarmigan Lake. This area is marshy in the wet season, and because of this, it is often filled with flowers. Another half mile brings you to Ptarmigan Lake at 12,132 feet.

To the right are the steep slopes of Jones Mountain and its ridge points extending to the north. The steep cliffs that you see to the

The Ptarmigan Lake trail as it winds through the forest.

left are off the Gladstone Ridge, which has an area on top called Big Grassy.

Ptarmigan Lake is popular for fishing, so you may find others here. Jones Mountain, at 13,218 feet, is the high point to the southwest. Directly to the south, and only about 150 feet above the lake, is a pass with a trail leading to Mineral Basin to the south.

There's a shorter walking route to Ptarmigan Lake for 4WD addicts. Driving the long route up Mineral Basin under good conditions can bring you to within a fairly short distance from the south side of the pass south of Ptarmigan Lake.

For the really venturesome, it is interesting to follow the old trail to Ptarmigan Lake. It provides quite a contrast with the new one

Meadow near the start of the Ptarmigan Lake trail.

described for this hike. The trailhead for the old trail is off the west side of the logging road that leads south from County 306 about three-fourths of a mile east of the trailhead for the newer trail.

This old trail is well marked with blazes on the trees, although the trail itself is sometimes difficult to follow. There is a fair amount of downed timber to be negotiated. The trail winds through the forest, generally following Ptarmigan Creek, and leads to the new trail near the first lakelet below Ptarmigan Lake. Following the old trail is recommended only for those experienced in route finding.

Recent logging in the area has diminished the beauty of this hike and has made the old trail practically unusable.

133

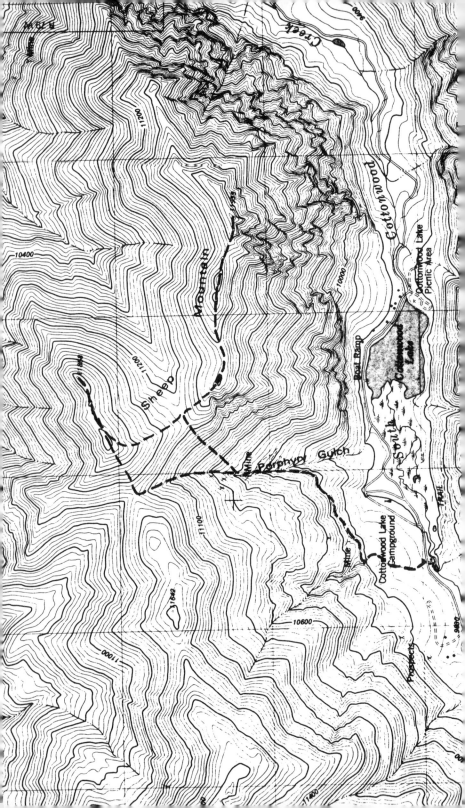

34. SHEEP MOUNTAIN

Distance: 5 miles (keyhole loop)
Starting elevation: 9,620 feet
High points: 11,939 feet and 11,858 feet
Elevation gain: 3,100 feet
Rating: difficult but short
Time allowed: 7 hours
Maps: 7.5 minute Mount Yale
San Isabel National Forest

The USGS reports that there are over thirty "Sheep" mountains in Colorado. This one deserves the name currently, since it has a resident population of bighorn sheep. We've seen them on every hike to this mountain, sometimes quite close.

The Sheep Mountain described here is in the Sawatch Range. From Buena Vista, its twin summits stand out between Mount Yale and Mount Princeton. While short, the climb of Sheep Mountain is more difficult than climbing either of its Fourteener neighbors.

From Buena Vista, take County 306 west, choosing the left fork at seven miles. Three more miles bring you to Cottonwood Lake. Circle the lake on the north, and pass south of Cottonwood Lake Campground. A quarter mile beyond the campground, find a 4WD road leading north in the vicinity of some old buildings. There is limited parking in this area.

Walk up this 4WD road, which is often closed to vehicles by a barrier. The road starts north and then turns east above and north of the campground. When the campground is directly below you, Sheep Mountain is directly ahead. This is a good place to start looking for bighorn sheep, which are frequently on the south-western cliffs of Sheep Mountain.

About a mile of hiking up the 4WD road brings you to a sharp turn left up Porphyry Gulch. Soon thereafter, you reach some private-property buildings and equipment at about 10,300 feet. Now the climb begins. Just beyond the building to the right of the 4WD road-end, head to the right up the steep slopes through the aspen. The objective is to reach the 11,260-foot saddle to the northeast between the two summits of Sheep Mountain. With no

Sheep Mountain as seen from Colorado 306 west of Buena Vista. The higher south summit is on the left, while the north summit is farther away to the right. The climbing route is on the other side of the summits.

trail, look for the least-steep sections and the most open route through the aspen. However, in the steepest sections the aspen are welcome, as they afford handholds and a way to pull yourself along.

Finally, you will emerge at the broad saddle between the two summits of Sheep Mountain. The 11,858-foot summit is to the left, and the higher, 11,939-foot summit is to the right.

Since this hike takes you to both summits, let's take the higher south summit first. Follow the broad ridge south, staying on top as the ridge narrows and bears to the east. The rest of the route is along the top of the ridge, through some brushy sections and over several rocky false summits. The last false summit leads to a 150-foot drop before the final climb to the true summit. The top affords a good view of the Middle and South Cottonwood Creek valley and the Arkansas River valley to the east.

Return to the saddle between the two summits of Sheep Mountain, and follow the ridge to the north. The ridge bears east and leads on

Approaching Sheep Mountain along the 4WD road, with a view of the cliffs where bighorn sheep are often seen.

to the north summit. This ridge is easier than the one to the south summit, but the view from the top' is just as outstanding.

After that steep climb through the aspen to the saddle, you'll no doubt be ready for a different descent route. So let's try one that's longer but not quite as steep. Return west along the ridge from the north summit. When the ridge that you came up on bears to the south, continue west. A 500-foot descent in less than a half mile brings you to an 11,300-foot saddle between Sheep Mountain and 13,209-foot Gladstone Ridge to the west. From this saddle, head directly south, following the steep drainage. Pick the easiest route through the timber and rocks to emerge at the end of the 4WD road.

This short hike is recommended for its varied terrain and excellent views from the top. However, it should not be attempted by those who dislike steep bushwhacking or who don't have a good sense of direction for off-trail hiking.

137

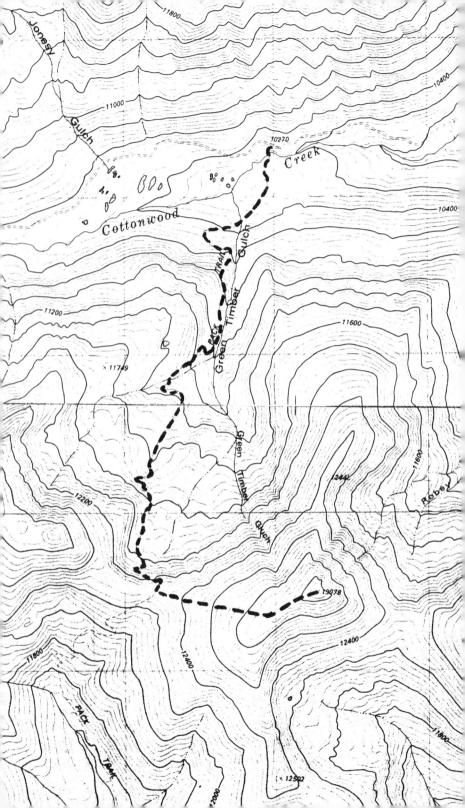

35. GREEN TIMBER GULCH AND PEAK 13,078

Distance: 8 miles (out and back)
Starting elevation: 10,270 feet
High point: 13,078 feet
Elevation gain: 2,800 feet
Rating: easy
Time allowed: 8 hours
Maps: 7.5 minute Mount Yale
7.5 minute St. Elmo
San Isabel National Forest

This is a very scenic hike on good trail, reaching an interesting unnamed pass, followed by an easy walk up the tundra to a remote high summit. In the early summer, there's a profusion of flowers both at the beginning and in the high meadows below the pass. The only drawback is that it is sometimes difficult to reach the trailhead with a standard car.

On County 306, go west seven miles from Buena Vista or 13 miles east from Cottonwood Pass. Turn south for three miles to Cottonwood Lake. Continue around the lake, past the Cottonwood Lake Campground. Hopefully, continue for three more miles along this road. Usually, 4WDs and smaller cars can make it, but there are several places that could stop larger cars. The trailhead is at a small clearing on the south side of the road. Look for a small lake and a trail crossing a bridge to the east and starting up the slope to the south. The trail should be easy to follow as it winds up Green Timber Gulch. It continues steadily upward as it leaves the timber to reach a pass at 12,300 feet.

From the pass, you can see down Poplar Gulch to the Chalk Creek valley below. Peak 13,078, east of the pass, is one of a string of summits along the ridge leading from Mount Princeton to the Continental Divide. It's an easy walk up the tundra slope to this summit.

With a car shuttle, a good point-to-point trip is possible. The continuation of the trail to the south down from the pass leads in three miles to the western edge of St. Elmo. However, that trail isn't as scenic as the one on the Green Timber Gulch side. If you don't have transportation waiting in St. Elmo, return the way you came.

Bridge at the start of the Green Timber Gulch trail.

Along the Green Timber Gulch trail.

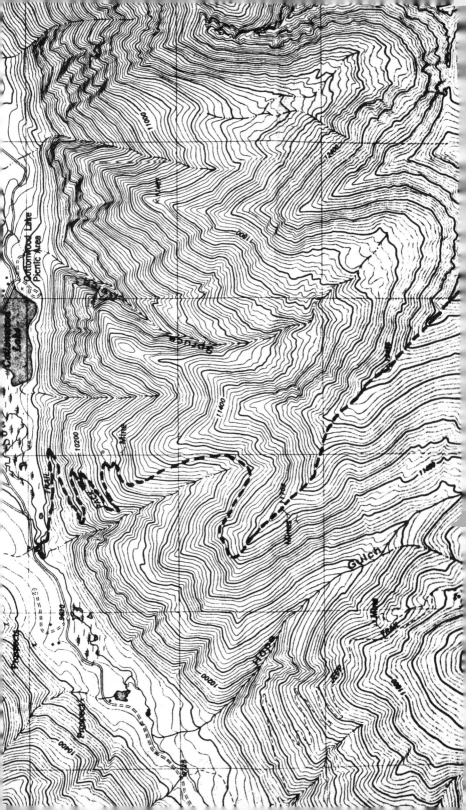

36. PEAK 13,626 ON MOUNT PRINCETON MASSIF

Distance: 10 miles (out and back)
Starting elevation: 9,600 feet
High point: 13,626 feet
Elevation gain: 4,100 feet
Rating: difficult
Time allowed: 10 hours
Maps: 7.5 minute Mount Yale
San Isabel National Forest

This hike is a route-finding adventure, utilizing an unmaintained and seldom-used trail that leads to a long ridge climb. Peak 13,626 is a separate summit northwest of and part of the Mount Princeton massif. It is much more difficult to reach than Mount Princeton, which is some 600 feet higher.

The trailhead is on the South Cottonwood Creek road, west of Cottonwood Lake. From Buena Vista, drive west on County 306 toward Cottonwood Pass. At seven miles, take the left fork for three miles to Cottonwood Lake. As the road passes Cottonwood Lake on the north and approaches Cottonwood Lake Campground beyond, notice the switchback trail on the mountainside to the south. That's our trail. Pass by the campground about a quarter of a mile, and seek a parking place near some buildings on the south side of the road.

Since the trail we'll be following is not maintained, there is no established starting point or surefire way of crossing South Cottonwood Creek to get to the start of it. Look for a log crossing near the buildings or along the creek toward Cottonwood Lake. If such a crossing can't be found, and if the water isn't dangerously high, it may be necessary to wade across. Once across the creek, the trail should be easy to locate as it starts climbing the hill to the left. After about a mile, the good-quality trail reaches a mine at 10,500 feet. From the mine, the trail switches back sharply to the west, rounds a ridge, and continues up the west side into a north-facing basin. It continues around the basin to reach another ridge at about 11,300 feet.

Switchback trail south of Cottonwood Lake, starting toward Peak 13,616 on the Mount Princeton massif.

At this point, the trail fades out, but it is no longer needed as the route is to the southeast up the ridge. Within a half mile, some buildings are passed, and another half mile brings you to timberline at about 12,000 feet. Continue to follow the crest of the ridge, which becomes rockier with less tundra. Don't be disheartened by the first big rock pile after leaving the tundra, as it's easier to negotiate than it looks. Getting higher, the ridge bears to the east, and the going gets slower over the rocks. There are no really difficult sections, but the large amount of climbing over the rocks adds to the total effort required.

Finally, the top is reached, and the entire side of the Mount Princeton massif comes into view. The ridge to the east leads to a point where it splits, the left segment going to the 13,451-foot summit that is so striking from the Cottonwood Pass road with its ragged ridge behind a deep basin. To the right is the ridge leading to 14,196-foot Mount Princeton by way of a 13,980-foot ridge point west of the summit.

It's best to return the same way, with the feeling that you've attained a remote and difficult summit, which probably hasn't had one climber for every thousand that have climbed nearby Mount Princeton.

If it is not safe to cross South Cottonwood Creek as described, there is an alternate starting point that avoids this crossing. Return east to the Cottonwood Lake Picnic Area on the southeast side of the lake. Hike west along the south side of the lake on fisherman trails and continue west on a path south of a swampy area. You will meet the hiking route south of South Cottonwood Creek where an old roadbed emerges from the creek. Turn left on this roadbed which is the beginning of the trail to the mine. Starting at the picnic area adds two miles to the hiking distance but may keep your feet dry.

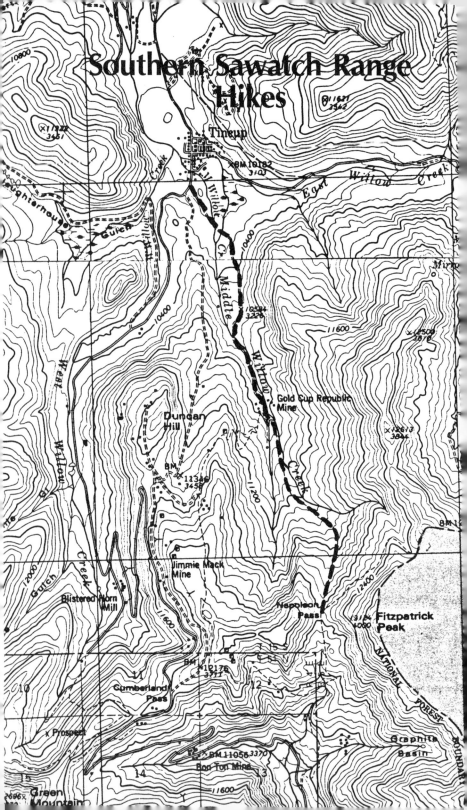

Southern Sawatch Range Hikes

37. NAPOLEON PASS

Distance: 10 miles (out and back)
Starting elevation: 10,200 feet
High point: 12,020 feet
Elevation gain: 2,000 feet
Rating: easy
Time allowed: 5 to 6 hours
Maps: 7.5 minute Cumberland Pass
Gunnison National Forest

The hike to Napoleon Pass explores some of the scenic country on the west side of the Continental Divide. Napoleon Pass is not a Continental Divide crossing but is on the ridge running west from the southern part of the Sawatch Range, leading to the Fossil Ridge area. The hike begins on an old road that becomes a rugged trail. This hike requires a long but scenic drive on unpaved roads to the trailhead. However, the drive gets you to a remote area where you are less likely to meet other hikers.

The starting point is just south of the town of Tincup, in the Taylor Park country. From Gunnison, follow Colorado 135 north for ten miles to Almont, then bear right and continue for twenty-three miles to Taylor Park. Or from Buena Vista follow County 306 over Cottonwood Pass and on down the western slope to Taylor Park. From Taylor Park, it's seven miles southeast on Forest Service Road 765 to Tincup.

A more scenic backroad route to Tincup starts a mile south of Monarch Pass on US 50. It crosses Old Monarch Pass, Black Sage Pass, Waunita Pass, and Cumberland Pass on the way to Tincup.

In Tincup, go south on the main street. At the southern edge of town, the main road turns from south to the southwest. At this point, find an old road leading southeast. This road can be driven for a short distance, but it's best to find the first suitable parking place.

Walk up this old road to the southeast. Within a half mile, there's a crossing of Middle Willow Creek. The old road bears to the east and after another mile returns to the west side of the

Looking north, down the valley, from Napoleon Pass.

creek. A bit over a half mile along the west side of the creek brings you to a large mining property.

Care should be taken to find the right trail at this point. South of the mine, cross a spur creek to the east, but stay on the west side of the main drainage of Middle Willow Creek. The route, now decidedly a trail, continues southeast along the west side of the creek for a mile. It then swings to the south, soon leaves the timber, and continues in open country to Napoleon Pass at 12,020 feet.

The high point to the east of Napoleon Pass is Fitzpatrick Peak, at 13,112 feet. Rugged Napoleon Mountain, a 12,563-foot summit, separates Napoleon Pass from the automobile road over Cumberland Pass. If you're lucky, you may be able to spot some of the resident mountain goats in this area.

The sketchy trail continues south from Napoleon Pass to eventually meet the road south of Cumberland Pass between Tincup and Pitkin. It would permit a good one-way hike with suitable transportation arrangements. Otherwise, return the way you came.

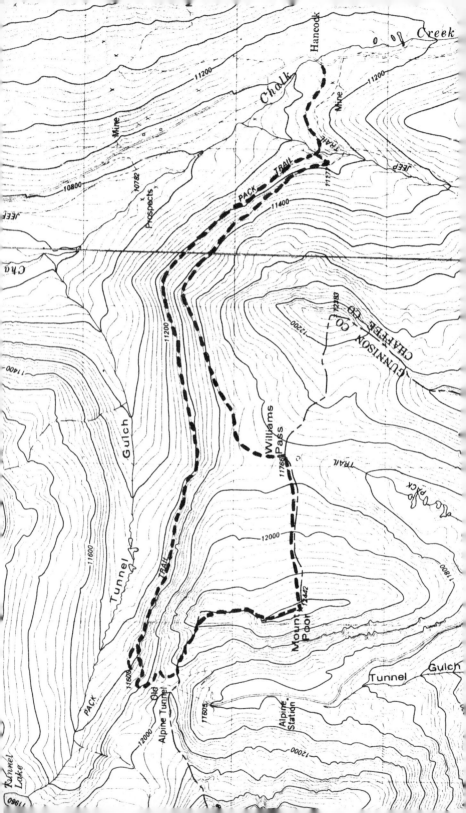

38. WILLIAMS PASS, MOUNT POOR, ALTMAN PASS, AND OLD ALPINE TUNNEL

Distance: 7 miles (loop)
Starting elevation: 11,040 feet
High point: 12,442 feet
Elevation gain: 1,500 feet
Rating: easy
Time allowed: 4 hours
Maps: 7.5 minute St. Elmo
   7.5 minute Cumberland Pass
  San Isabel National Forest
  Gunnison National Forest

This hike takes you from an old ghost town to a Continental Divide pass, across a newly named mountain, to a pass above an historic railroad tunnel under the divide, and back along the roadbed of a short-lived narrow-gauge railroad.

The starting point is at the ghost town of Hancock. At Nathrop, on US 285, turn west on County 162. Follow the paved road for nine miles, then a good gravel road for six and one-half miles to a "Y" junction before reaching St. Elmo. Turn left on Chaffee County 295, bypassing St. Elmo, and follow this lesser-quality road five and one-half miles to the ghost town of Hancock. Hancock is reached shortly after a spectacular view of triangular Sewanee Peak is seen directly ahead. The road curves to the right of abandoned buildings in a flat clearing at Hancock.

Park at what is the end of the auto road at a junction of two 4WD roads, one continuing west and the other turning south. The first part of the hike is on the 4WD road to Williams Pass. Walk up the 4WD road leading west and look for another fork within a quarter of a mile. Take the left road at this fork, following the road as it parallels the right fork at a slightly higher level. Continue on this 4 WD road for a mile to Williams Pass at 11,766 feet. Williams Pass is a flat, swampy area that is often too wet for vehicles to cross, even those with 4WD.

Proceed up the gentle tundra slope to the west, bearing to the left part of the long flat summit ahead. The high point is at the extreme south end of the summit area.

Old building perched above the road to Hancock.

From the summit, you can get the first view of the remains of the station of the Denver, South Park and Pacific Railroad, at the west portal of the Old Alpine Tunnel. The tunnel was built in 1882 and abandoned in 1910. The 12,442-foot mountain that you're standing on for this view, Mount Poor, was only recently named. Its name is in honor of M.C. Poor, the historian who devoted much effort to compiling the history of the Old Alpine Tunnel.

From the summit, head north along the ridge and descend to Altman Pass, the unofficially named point above the tunnel at 11,940 feet. For a side trip, you can descend 350 feet on easy slopes to the west side of the Continental Divide, which is southerly at this point, to visit the railroad relics below. If you make this side trip, return to Altman Pass.

From Altman Pass, find a trail leading down to the east portal of the tunnel. There isn't as much to see on this side, as the tunnel is caved in and usually filled with snow.

From the east portal of the tunnel, the route follows the old railroad grade for three and one-half miles back to Hancock. This has been used as a 4WD road, but some remains of the railroad ties can be seen. The route meets the one that you followed to Williams Pass just before reaching Hancock.

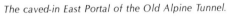

The caved-in East Portal of the Old Alpine Tunnel.

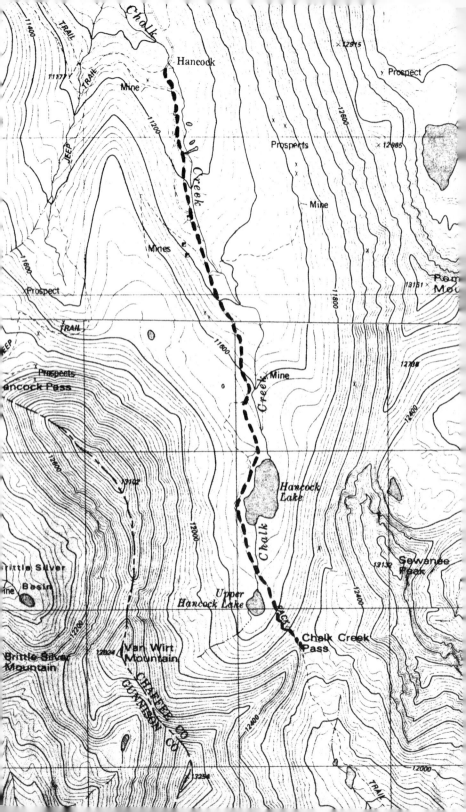

39. HANCOCK LAKE AND CHALK CREEK PASS

Distance: 7 miles (out and back)
Starting elevation: 11,040 feet
High point: 12,140 feet
Elevation gain: 1,100 feet
Rating: easy
Time allowed: 5 hours
Maps: 7.5 minute Garfield
7.5 minute St. Elmo
San Isabel National Forest

This trip begins with a pleasant walk to a lake set in a scenic cirque just east of the Continental Divide. Then there's a trail through the open country to a higher lake. From there, the route is up easy slopes to an historic pass set between two rugged mountains.

The starting point is the same as for the hike to Williams Pass and the Old Alpine Tunnel, so follow the directions to the parking area in Hancock as described in hike number 38. This time, walk up the 4WD road that leads south from the parking area. Within a hundred yards, there's a junction with a 4WD road leading off to the right and up the hill. The road to the right leads to Hancock Pass, a difficult 4WD crossing of the Continental Divide. Our route takes the left fork to continue from this junction south past mine buildings and then through the timber. This part of the route is often wet, sometimes making it impassable for vehicles. A mile and a half through the woods bring you to open country, with good views of the mountainous cirque surrounding Hancock Lake. It's a short half mile with very little elevation gain to the sizable Hancock Lake at 11,660 feet.

Hancock Lake is often well populated with fishermen, so you may find some company here. Continue on either side of the lake, following the trails to past an even more scenic upper lake. Beyond the upper lake, the trail leads up easy switchbacks on grassy slopes to Chalk Creek Pass, which is only 500 feet above the upper lake.

The head of the valley is dominated by a 13,254-foot ridge point to the right of Chalk Creek Pass. To the north of this ridge point is 13,024-foot Van Wirt Mountain, and north along that ridge is an

Sewanee Peak as seen from the trail to Hancock Lake. The climbing route is on the other side of the mountain.

unnamed 13,102-foot summit. To the left is Sewanee Peak. Viewed from this side, Sewanee Peak appears to be not nearly as formidable as the first view that you get when driving into Hancock. While Sewanee Peak can be climbed from Chalk Creek Pass, we prefer the approach from the east—a more interesting climb that is described in hike number 42.

The trail descends from Chalk Creek Pass to the south into the valley of the Middle Fork of the Arkansas River. Various possibilities exist for a point-to-point hike or loop trip. With transportation arranged, you could descend into the valley of the Middle Fork and in five to six miles emerge at Garfield on US 50.

Another possibility is a climb westward up the ridge to the 13,254-foot ridge point. From there, the slow ridge can be followed north to Van Wirt Mountain, over the unnamed 13,102-foot summit, and then down to Hancock Pass. From Hancock Pass, a 4WD road leads down to Hancock.

However, we've described this hike as an out-and-back venture, so the suggested return is by the way you came.

156

Under the best conditions, this hike can be shortened by about a mile with regular cars and by three and one-half miles with 4WD. A barrier stops all vehicles a quarter mile short of the lake.

Looking across Hancock Lake at Chalk Creek Pass.

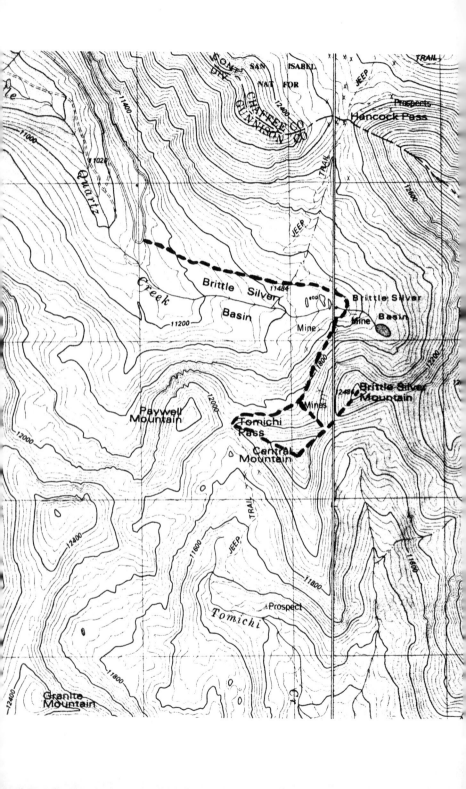

40. TOMICHI PASS, CENTRAL MOUNTAIN, AND BRITTLE SILVER MOUNTAIN

Distance: 4 miles (keyhole loop)
Starting elevation: 11,100 feet
High point: 12,486 feet
Elevation gain: 1,800 feet
Rating: easy
Time allowed: 4 hours
Maps: 7.5 minute Garfield
*   7.5 minute Whitepine*
*   Gunnison National Forest*

Tomichi Pass crosses a spur ridge that extends west from the southern part of the Sawatch Range. It is regarded as a hairy 4WD road and has been the scene of serious accidents in past years. It makes a better hike. Tomichi Pass is in a remote area where you're not too likely to find other hikers. The hike can be combined with an auto trip to the west portal of the Old Alpine Tunnel to see the relics that are displayed there. That's an alternate to visiting the west portal as part of hike number 38.

There are various ways to reach the trailhead, but the best one for regular cars is off of US 50. At Parlin, twelve miles east of Gunnison or fifty-three miles west of Salida on US 50, turn northeast toward Pitkin. The road is paved to Pitkin, and then an unpaved road continues east. Follow this unpaved road for about two and one-half miles to Forest Service Road 839, which is called the Alpine Tunnel road. Take road 839 to the right, and make a sharp turn to the south. The road turns east after a mile and stays on the north side of Middle Quartz Creek.

After seven and one-half miles, the road swings south and then makes a sharp "U"-turn to the north. Just at the sharp turn to the north, find a 4WD road leading to the east. Consider this the trailhead and pick out a good parking place. With a 4WD vehicle, good conditions, and more than average courage, the trailhead area can be reached from the east over Hancock Pass.

The beginning of a 4WD road, which is the trailhead for the hike to Tomichi Pass.

From the trailhead, follow the 4WD road to the east. Within three-quarters of a mile, a road to the left leads uphill to Hancock Pass. Continue straight ahead, and soon make a sharp turn to the right. The old road soon becomes a shelf road with steep drop-offs to the right. It's through here that the route was once described as a "terrifying wagon road," and more recently it has been about as terrifying for some 4WD enthusiasts.

A short stretch along the shelf road brings you to a sharp left turn and soon thereafter to Tomichi Pass. There's a good view into the Tomichi Creek basin to the south. Somewhere down there was once a town of Tomichi, which was wiped out by an avalanche in 1899.

Since it was such a short and easy walk to Tomichi Pass, we suggest a return over two small mountains. The first, 12,380-foot Central Mountain, is a short ridge walk up the slopes to the east. After this climb of a bit over 400 feet, descend about 300 feet into the saddle to the northeast.

The next objective, Brittle Silver Mountain, is a western spur off of Van Wirt Mountain. Continue northeast with a climb of about 400 feet to the 12,486-foot summit of Brittle Silver Mountain. The descent for the return route is easier if you go back to the saddle between Brittle Silver Mountain and Central Mountain. Then go down through the valley toward the northwest to reach the shelf road. The entire trip across Central and Brittle Silver mountains is easy walking on mostly grassy tundra slopes.

After returning to the trailhead, you may want to visit the west portal of the Old Alpine Tunnel. If so, drive north on the road from Pitkin for another three miles beyond our trailhead. Sometimes this road is in questionable condition. You may want to inquire in Pitkin on its condition, and also on the status of the exhibits at the Old Alpine Tunnel. The drive from Pitkin to the Old Alpine Tunnel is glorious when the aspen have turned golden.

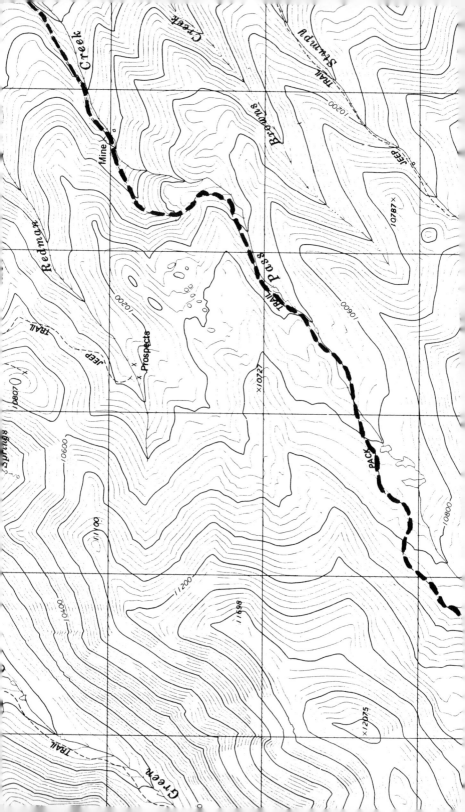

41. PASS CREEK LAKE

Distance: 10 miles (out and back)
Starting elevation: 9,220 feet
High point: 11,340 feet
Elevation gain: 2,200 feet
Rating: easy
Time allowed: 6 hours
Maps: 7.5 minute Mount Ouray
San Isabel National Forest

Take a hike along a good trail to a beautiful lake surrounded by forest. When such a hike starts from near a major highway, you'd expect it to be a popular hiking route. Surprisingly, for such a nice hiking trail and scenic destination, you're not likely to find other hikers in the area. This is an especially good hike for the fall, when the aspen are turning color.

To find the trailhead, follow US 50 two miles west of Poncha Springs, fifteen and one-half miles east of Monarch Pass. Here, a road, Chaffee County 210, leads south, which is the entry both to the Pass Creek and Little Cochetopa Creek trails. At 1.3 miles, take the right fork, Chaffee County 212, and continue on this road past ranch lands.

After two miles of good gravel road, the right fork leads up the hill along the right side of a fence line. The road here becomes rockier and narrower, with some steep climbs. Less than a mile brings you to a gate, and another quarter mile to a junction of four roads. Take the left road for a couple of hundred yards to park in a level wooded area. This is the trailhead. Only 4WD vehicles should try to go further, and under good conditions, a 4WD might make another mile and a half.

Walk along the 4WD road, which in a mile brings you to several old mine buildings. Continue on the 4WD road beyond these buildings for a half mile, where the road abruptly ends and a good-quality trail continues.

The trail climbs the hillside to the north of Pass Creek. Within a mile, it nears the creek again and follows a scenic route on the north side. Beaver ponds are numerous in this area, with some spectacularly large beaver dams. After one brief stretch on the

Old mine buildings along the trail to Pass Creek Lake.

south side of the creek, the trail returns to the north side. It again crosses to the south side for a final short approach to the lake.

Unlike the many high lakes in the Sawatch Range that are above timberline, Pass Creek Lake is set in a heavily wooded area. You can get brief glimpses through the trees of the vast cirque in which the lake sits. The steep slopes to the southwest lead to a 13,472-foot unnamed summit north of Chipeta Mountain.

The lake is surrounded by large rocks, including some flat ones that make good stopping places for lunch. After relaxing at the lake, the return is by the same route.

Large beaver dam along the trail to Pass Creek Lake.

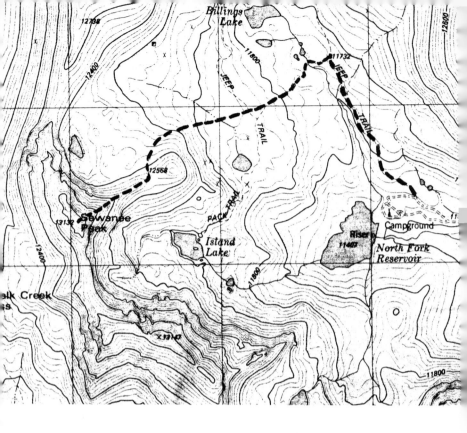

42. SEWANEE PEAK

Distance: 5 miles (out and back)
Starting elevation: 11,480 feet
High point: 13,132 feet
Elevation gain: 1,700 feet
Rating: moderate, with route finding on a difficult-
   looking ridge
Time allowed: 4 hours
Maps: 7.5 minute Garfield
          San Isabel National Forest

When you approach Sewanee Peak on the road from St. Elmo to
Hancock, it looks like a difficult technical climb. When you look at
it from Chalk Creek Pass, it appears to be a lot easier. From Billings

Lake to the east of Sewanee, the ridge route appears to be somewhere between these other two in difficulty. However, when you hike it, this route proves to be easier. It's recommended only for those who enjoy searching out the easiest route on a difficult-looking ridge. We think that this hike is the best way to get to Sewanee Peak, and the most interesting one, besides. You also get to explore an interesting basin circled by a high ridge, with a large lake and mine relics.

To reach the trailhead, follow the North Fork of the South Arkansas River. Drive to Maysville on US 50, which is six miles west of Poncha Springs, or eleven and one-half miles east of Monarch Pass. Turn north on a good gravel road that passes Shavano Campground in six miles. Beyond the campground, the road deteriorates somewhat, but it is normally passable for another two miles to a junction. Here, the left fork goes to the North Fork Reservoir Campground, but we want to take the right fork. Since the right fork is often passable only by 4WD vehicles, consider that road junction the trailhead, and find suitable parking there.

Walk on up this right fork on the 4WD road for almost a mile to enter a large basin. Large Billings Lake dominates the flat area of the basin. After reaching the open area and when within sight of Billings Lake, leave the road and head west over the open area. Continue west up the gradual slope, and then bear somewhat south, staying on the north side of the northeast ridge of Sewanee Peak. After reaching a point alongside the ridge, turn sharply left to climb to a small saddle separating a 12,568-foot ridge point from the main bulk of Sewanee Peak.

From this point, the route is directly up the ridge to the southwest. A look at the ridge would tell you that such a route would be a difficult climb. But interestingly enough, it is not nearly as difficult as it looks. Just start up the ridge and look for the easiest walking route. Sometimes you may reach a dead end and have to try another route, but in each case there's a way that's not too difficult. It's best to stay near the top of the ridge all the way to the summit.

From Sewanee Peak, there's a good view of Hancock Lake to the west, looking down the sheer side of Sewanee Peak. Chalk Creek Pass is off to the southwest. To the north is Pomeroy Mountain, and to the right of that is unofficially named Pomeroy Pass. It is a rocky climb over Pomeroy Pass into Pomeroy Gulch on the other side.

When you're ready to return, pick your way back along the ridge, to descend by the same route on which you came.

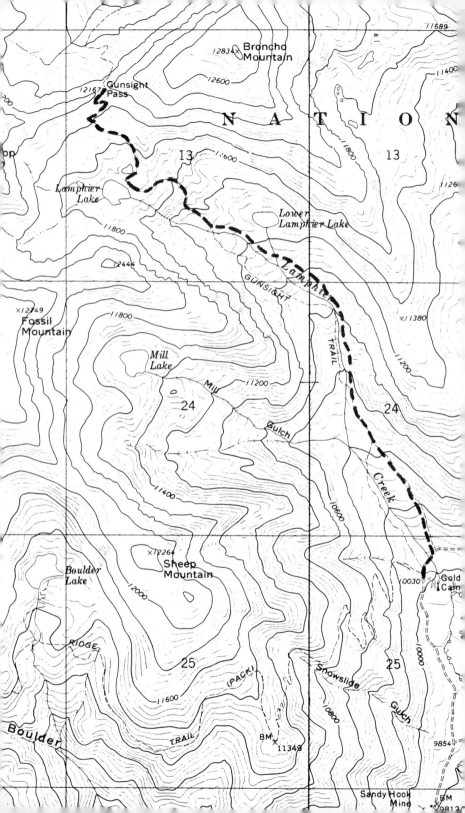

43. GUNSIGHT PASS

> Distance: 7 miles (out and back)
> Starting elevation: 10,030 feet
> High point: 12,167 feet
> Elevation gain: 2,200 feet
> Rating: easy
> Time allowed: 5 hours
> Maps: 7.5 minute Fairview Peak
>   Gunnison National Forest

There are at least four "Gunsight" passes in Colorado. This Gunsight Pass is in the Fossil Ridge area, a westward extension from the southern part of the Sawatch Range. This one provides an enjoyable hike, mostly on good trail, with outstanding scenery and a spectacular view when the objective is reached.

Other passes named "Gunsight" are in the Crested Butte area, the San Juan Mountains near Wolf Creek Pass, and the Rabbit Ears Pass area near Steamboat Springs. However, none fit the name better than this one. The trailhead for this hike to Gunsight Pass is in an area remote from main highways. This helps make the hike more enjoyable because it is in a less-used area.

The trailhead is at Gold Creek Campground, north of Ohio City. Ohio City may be reached from US 50 between Gunnison and Monarch Pass. Drive to Parlin, which is twelve miles east of Gunnison, or fifty-three miles west of Salida. Turn northeast at Parlin on paved road toward Pitkin, which follows Quartz Creek. Drive about ten miles to Ohio City. At Ohio City, take Gunnison County Road 771 along Gold Creek, and follow this good-quality unpaved road about seven miles north. This brings you to Gold Creek Campground, which is on the right-hand side of the road. This small campground provides good camping and ample parking space for hikers.

The trailhead can also be reached from Pitkin. You may get to Pitkin from US 50, from a mile east of Monarch Pass, Black Sage Pass, and Waunita Pass. Pitkin can also be reached from the Taylor Park area, over Cumberland Pass. From Pitkin, follow the route through Ohio City to Gold Creek Campground.

To find the trailhead, walk up the road past the trail leading westward up the slope across from the campground. Do not take that nearby trail, as it is the lengthy Fossil Ridge Trail, leading westward. Instead, walk northeast along the road, past the Fossil Ridge trailhead about 100 yards, crossing Lamphier Creek on a bridge. The trailhead for Gunsight Pass is just beyond this bridge, on the left. It starts out as an old road, leading north.

The trail follows gentle grades, generally near Lamphier Creek, all the way to Lamphier Lake, at 11,700 feet. A first short portion is a 4WD road that could be driven, but that is not really necessary on a hike of this type. As the trail ascends through the timber, it generally stays east and northeast of Lamphier Creek. At about the two-mile point, it crosses the outlet from Lower Lamphier Lake. Lower Lamphier Lake is close by, but not visible from the trail.

Soon thereafter, more gentle gradients are reached as the trail approaches Lamphier Lake. This rather large lake is set in a basin surrounded by the cliffs of Fossil Mountain to the south and Square Top Mountain to the west. Don't rely on the USGS 7½ minute Fairview Peak quadrangle, dated 1967, to show the exact route of the trail. However, the trail does follow Lamphier Creek all the way to the lake.

Beyond the lake, the trail is indistinct in spots, but the objective is obvious. Gunsight Pass is the low point on the ridge to the north. It is framed by the steep slopes of Broncho Mountain to the east and the rough, ragged ridge leading to Square Top Mountain to the west. As the trail breaks out of the timber to cross the meadows north of Lamphier Lake, some large posts help mark the way. The trail soon enters a rocky area and takes some switchbacks leading up the steep slopes below the pass.

Upon arrival at the pass, you realize why the name "Gunsight" was chosen. The narrow pass, with steep cliffs on each side, provides a sharp contrast to the broad expanses of many Colorado passes. The view to the north down the long Brush Creek valley is striking. The sight of the narrow, rocky trail winding its way down to the valley far below brings out the reason why a sign is often found at the trailhead stating "no horses beyond Gunsight Pass."

Many hikers, upon reaching a pass, consider the possibilities of climbing the mountains on either side. In this case, Broncho Mountain, to the east, is possible to climb by contouring southeast, ascending the steep, rocky slopes, and continuing on the easier and more gentle slopes above. In contrast, following the ridge westward to Square Top Mountain, 12,985 feet, would be a much more difficult matter. The ragged ridge, with its many towers and spires, would cause most hikers to choose another route to reach Square Top.

An interesting one-way hike over Gunsight Pass is possible if suitable transportation arrangements can be made. Continuing north from the pass, the trail descends to Brush Creek and follows it and South Lottis Creek to emerge at the Lottis Creek Campground. The Lottis Creek Campground is on the road between Taylor Park and Gunnison.

It's roughly twelve miles of hiking from the Gold Creek Campground to the Lottis Creek Campground. By car, the trip between these campgrounds is some fifty miles, either through Gunnison or Pitkin.

The trail to Gunsight Pass from Gold Creek Campground usually is reasonably free of snow by June. However, the one-way trip is best made later, since snow often covers the trail north of the pass until midsummer.

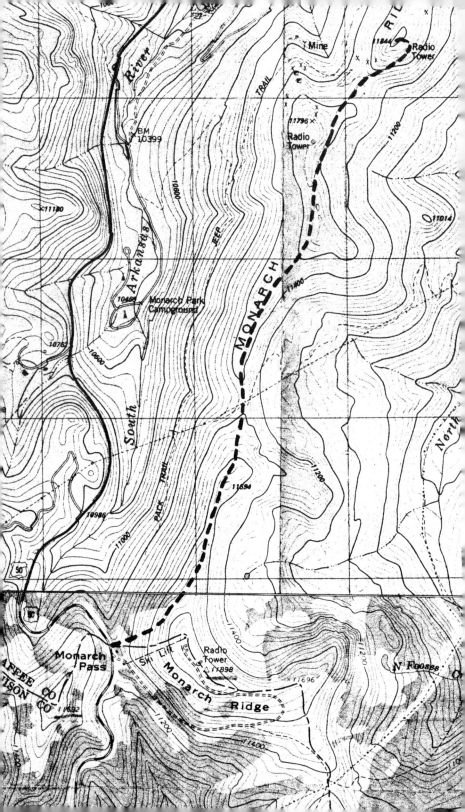

44. MONARCH RIDGE

Distance: 5½ miles (out and back)
Starting elevation: 11,300 feet
High point: 11,844 feet
Elevation gain: 1,900 feet
Rating: easy
Time allowed: 4 hours
Maps: 7.5 minute Garfield
7.5 minute Pahlone Peak
San Isabel National Forest

This off-trail hike provides a bit of steep climbing, interesting ridge walking above timberline, and excellent views—all starting from a popular main highway pass and without venturing into altitudes above 12,000 feet.

Start the hike at Monarch Pass, on US 50 between Gunnison and Salida. From the parking area on the east side of the highway, go around the north end of the buildings, and head up the hill to the east. Keep generally to the left of the gondola, staying above the heavy timber on the left after breaking out into the open area. Gain the crest of the ridge at a point north of and somewhat lower than the gondola summit house.

After climbing to about 11,700 feet, you'll go down to reach an 11,376-foot saddle. Then it's up to 11,740- and 11,796-foot ridge points. Most of the ridge is quite broad and some parts are sparsely forested, so it's easy to find your way along the ridge crest. Through this section, you'll be able to see the large quarry and mine down the hill to the west.

The high point at the end of the ridge, at 11,844 feet, is another three-fourths of a mile further. As you approach this summit point, you can follow a road to the right of the ridge. From a point opposite the summit, climb up the rocky slope to the top.

The view to the north from the summit is of 13,651-foot Taylor Mountain on the right and 13,745-foot Mount Aetna to the left. The unique rock slide, dropping almost 3,000 feet off Mount Aetna's south side, is the most striking feature of this northern view.

Return along the ridge the same way you came.

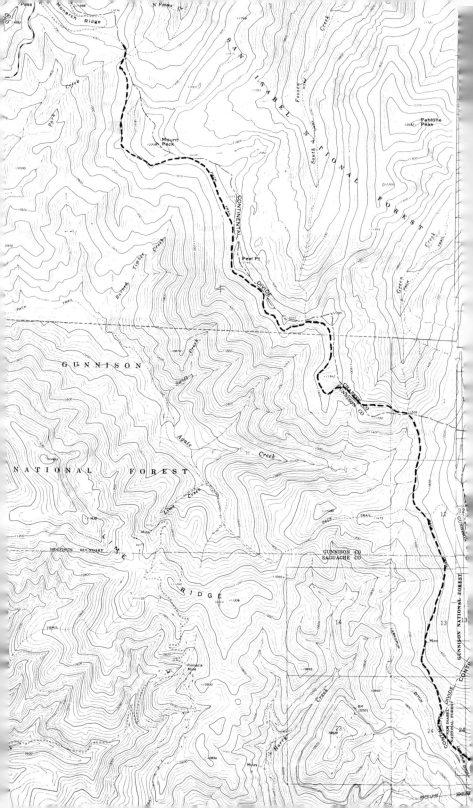

45. MONARCH PASS TO MARSHALL PASS

Distance: 11 miles (point-to-point)
Starting elevation: 11,300 feet
High point: 11,940 feet
Elevation gain: 1,000 feet
Rating: easy
Time allowed: 7 hours
Maps: 7.5 minute Pahlone Peak
 7.5 minute Mount Ouray
 San Isabel National Forest
 Gunnison National Forest

This hike is described as a point-to-point venture and thus would take a car shuttle to complete. However, if such transportation is not available, half or more of the hike can be taken by starting either at Monarch Pass or Marshall Pass. The hike is entirely on trail that stays on or near the crest of the Continental Divide.

For a one-way hike, you need to spot a car or arrange for pickup at Marshall Pass, 10,860 feet. Marshall Pass may be reached from the east on good gravel road by turning west from US 285, six miles south of Poncha Springs. To reach Marshall Pass from the west, turn south from Sargents, on US 50 between Gunnison and Monarch Pass, for the sixteen-mile unpaved route to the pass.

The hike begins from the Monarch Pass parking area on US 50 between Gunnison and Salida. Start up the service road that goes southeasterly under the gondola. Within a quarter of a mile, a trail, not shown on the topographic map, contours off to the right. This trail leads to a saddle crossed by a power line at 11,380 feet. At this point, a trail goes down the slope to the east, to follow North Fooses Creek.

The trail we want to follow goes uphill on the west side of the ridge. It continues on the right side of the ridge to contour around 12,208-foot Mount Peck. After reaching a Continental Divide saddle beyond Mount Peck, it continues on the west side of the divide, sometimes very near the top.

After rounding the south side of Peel Point, the trail heads east to reach another saddle at 11,900 feet, from which the South Fooses Creek Trail takes off to the north. At this point, an unnamed 12,195-foot summit is directly east.

Mount Peck, viewed along the trail from Monarch Pass to Marshall Pass. (photo by Gordon McKeague)

A broad saddle along the route from Monarch Pass to Marshall Pass. (photo by Gordon McKeague)

To the north and slightly east is Pahlone Peak, at 12,667 feet. If you wanted to include Pahlone Peak on your trip, this would be the starting point for the climb.

Continuing on our trail, you'll round one ridge point to the west and then go on the east side of another to reach a saddle from which the Green Creek Trail enters the valley to the north. Our trail now heads directly south, staying west of the Continental Divide. It soon crosses another trail that comes up from Agate Creek to the west and goes on down Little Cochetopa Creek to the east. Our trail continues south along the flank of 13,971-foot Mount Ouray. A little further on, the trail becomes a 4WD road, returns to the Continental Divide, and leads on down to Marshall Pass.

If you are starting from Marshall Pass, pick up the route somewhat east of the pass. Avoid the 4WD road that starts just west of the pass and that leads along Larkspur Ditch. If you're on that road by mistake, it'll take some uphill bushwhacking to get back to the proper trail.

The hike provides good views along most of the way. The drive to historic Marshall Pass, whichever approach is used, is also interesting. There's a descent of almost 500 feet between Monarch Pass and Marshall Pass, and the uphill and downhill sections of the hike are well distributed. For those with only a short time to spend hiking from Monarch Pass, a portion of the route makes a nice hike.

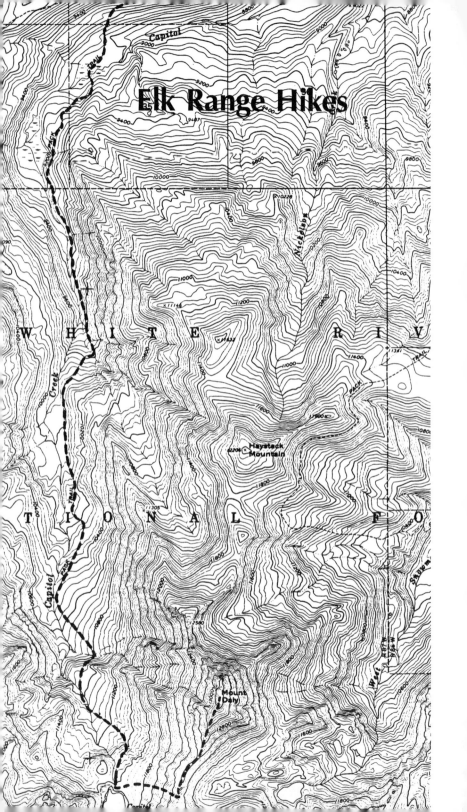

Elk Range Hikes

46. CAPITOL LAKE AND MOUNT DALY

Distance: 17 miles (out and back)
Starting elevation: 9,400 feet
High point: 13,300 feet
Elevation gain: 4,700 feet
Rating: difficult, because of the distance and elevation
  gain
Time allowed: 10 to 12 hours
Maps: 7.5 minute Capitol Peak
    White River National Forest

Capitol Peak is one of the more difficult climbs of the Colorado Fourteeners. Ordinarily, this climb requires an overnight pack-in to Capitol Lake. Many climbers may not really appreciate the scenic route to Capitol Lake when thinking about the Capitol Peak climb the next day. Our hike takes us to Mount Daly, a 13,300-foot summit on the ridge north of Capitol Peak. This hike, while a long one, can be done in a day. It combines a trip to the scenic lake with a steep climb to an easy-to-reach summit.

The trailhead is reached from Colorado 82 between Aspen and Glenwood Springs. Go fourteen miles west of Aspen, or twenty-eight miles east of Glenwood Springs to the town of Snowmass. Turn south for two miles, take the right fork, and continue southwest for another seven and one-half miles, which is one and one-half miles beyond the Capitol Creek Guard Station. At this point, the road is on the south side of a steep hill, and there is parking space near where several trails lead to the south.

Walk down a trail to the south as it descends about 400 feet into the Capitol Creek valley. Here, a crossing must be made to the east side of the creek. If there is no bridge in place, crossing may be difficult. Look for the best of several possible log or brush crossings. The excellent trail on the east side of the creek climbs steadily but not steeply through the scenic forest area. There are stretches in the open country, and after about six miles, timberline is reached at 11,100 feet. Here, the impressive northwest face of Capitol Peak comes into view. Down the ridge from Capitol Peak, to the left, is Mount Daly, our objective.

Capitol Peak from the trail to Capitol Lake. (photo by Bill Bueler)

Capitol Peak, the high point on the left, and Mount Daly to its right, as seen from the ridge near Buckskin Pass. (photo by Bill Bueler)

Mount Daly, as seen from the ridge to Capitol Peak. (photo by Art Tauchen)

Continue on the trail to cross a small rise that brings the first view of Capitol Lake. This lake is large and impressive set against the steep west face of Capitol Peak. The trail that you have followed continues around the west side of the lake, crosses a pass, and descends into the Avalanche Creek valley. After viewing Capitol Lake, we leave the trail to head directly up the slopes to the east, making for an obvious pass to the north of Capitol Peak. There are many trails of use to help in climbing the steep slopes. A climb of 900 feet in less than a half mile brings you to a broad saddle at 12,500 feet.

So far we've followed the route of climbers of Capitol Peak, but here the routes diverge. Capitol Peak climbers turn right; Mount Daly is directly up the ridge to the north, or to the left. Generally, the route follows the ridge, bypassing some obvious rocky parts. The ridge is not as steep as the climb to the pass, with an altitude gain of 800 feet over three-fourths of a mile.

From the top of Mount Daly, besides the impressive view of Capitol Peak to the south, there are the Maroon Bells to the southeast. Mount Sopris can be seen standing alone to the northwest. While it would be possible to descend off the west side of Mount Daly, it's best to return the way you came.

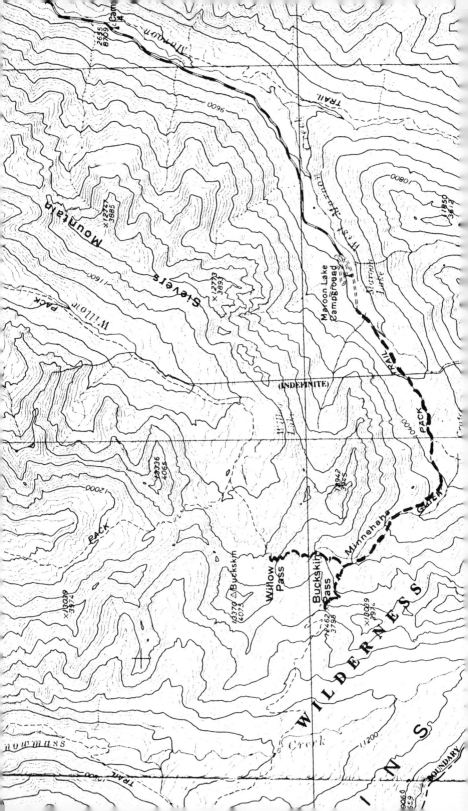

47. BUCKSKIN PASS AND WILLOW PASS

Distance: 11 miles (out and back)
Starting elevation: 9,580 feet
High point: 12,580 feet
Elevation gain: 3,900 feet
Rating: moderate, all trail, but large elevation gain
Time allowed: 9 hours
Maps: 7.5 minute Maroon Bells
*   White River National Forest*

No book on hikes in the Elk Range would be complete without the hike to Buckskin Pass. It's the perfect illustration of why hiking to a pass is often more dramatic than climbing a mountain. When you reach a pass, the view on the other side unfolds all at once. No view is more impressive than the spectacular sight of Snowmass Mountain and the surrounding area when you reach Buckskin Pass. The one disadvantage is that you won't be alone. There are usually lots of people at the trailhead and along this popular trail. This hike also includes a trip to Willow Pass, another pass in the same general area but one that offers completely different scenic views. Either of these passes makes a fine trip, but we hope that you have time for both.

The trailhead is at Maroon Lake, popular tourist spot for ogling the Maroon Bells. From Colorado 82 a half mile west of Castle Creek bridge in Aspen, follow the paved road nine and one-half miles south to the parking area. If you want to make this drive yourself, rather than park near Aspen and ride a bus, check on the hours that the road is open to private vehicles.

No trail description is really needed for this popular hike on good-quality trail, as you just follow the crowd. The points of decision are at one and one-half miles, where you take a right fork before getting to Crater Lake, and at three and one-half miles, where the left fork goes toward Buckskin and the right fork goes to Willow Pass. About a mile beyond Crater Lake, you'll pass a trail leading off to the left, where climbers of North Maroon Peak leave the main trail to head for the basin below the north face.

From the parking area, the route leads along the west side of Maroon Lake. There are several trails in the area, but the proper one is the main trail toward Crater Lake.

As you approach Crater Lake, there are several paths leading off to the left, so stay to the right to keep on the route toward Buckskin and Willow Passes. The trail junction after three and one-half miles is in a relatively flat area beyond the timber. Buckskin Pass is in plain view to the west. The left fork will take you to Buckskin Pass, and we'll assume that you want to go there first. Continue up this trail, which brings you to the pass on steep switchbacks.

No words can add to the sight that you'll see when you reach Buckskin Pass. Magnificent Snowmass Mountain dominates the scene to the west, with rugged Capitol Peak to the right of it. The trail continues beyond Buckskin Pass to reach Snowmass Lake, a favorite trip for backpackers. The trip from Buckskin Pass to Willow Pass may be an anticlimax, but we suggest that trip also, since Willow Pass is so near.

It's only a bit more than a half mile from Buckskin Pass to Willow Pass, with a net elevation gain of about 100 feet. However, the trail route is suggested, which is about two miles with an 800-foot elevation gain. Return to the trail junction previously described, and turn left on the trail heading northeast. This trail snakes

Approaching Willow Pass on a snow-covered trail.

around a ridge and heads into a large basin as Willow Pass comes into view. The final climb to the pass is on long and steep switchbacks.

From Willow Pass, there's a good view of the large Willow Lake to the right in the valley to the east and strings of rugged unnamed peaks on each side of the valley. The prime view from Willow Pass is to the south up West Maroon Creek. This valley is surrounded by impressive summits.

The route back is down the trail to the junction with the Buckskin Pass Trail and on back the way you came.

Maroon Bells from the ridge between Buckskin Pass and Willow Pass. (photo by Bill Bueler)

48. WEST MAROON PASS

Distance: 13 miles (out and back)
Starting elevation: 9,580 feet
High point: 12,500 feet
Elevation gain: 3,000 feet
Rating: moderate, long, but all on trail
Time allowed: 8 to 9 hours
Maps: 7.5 minute Maroon Bells
White River National Forest

This scenic hike follows part of the route used by backpackers for a several-day trip around the Maroon Bells. The route follows the valley between the Maroons and another Fourteener, Pyramid Peak. It's on good trail all the way.

The trailhead is the same as for the hike to Buckskin Pass and Willow Pass, so follow the description of how to get there for hike number 47. Hike south for a mile and a half to the trail junction, where the right fork goes to Buckskin and Willow passes. Bear to the left and follow any one of several trails leading south toward Crater Lake. It's best to stay as close to the west side of Crater Lake as the water level permits. South of the lake, you'll return to a single trail that continues all the way to West Maroon Pass.

As you proceed south, take a look to the right at the several routes up to the ridge south of Maroon Peak. These routes, which are used in climbing and descending the Maroons, are successively easier as you continue south. However, the farther south a climber goes, the longer the trip, so some opt for the harder routes.

To the left is the impressive ridge leading south from Pyramid Peak, and about a mile south of Crater Lake is the takeoff point for a climb of 13,932-foot Thunder Peak, on the ridge south of Pyramid Peak.

For the last mile or so, the trail leaves the West Maroon Creek valley and climbs out of the timber. As you cross this open country, look to the right to see the trail carved into the side of the steep ridge as it approaches the pass. This is the route you'll follow.

From the pass, the trail continues east into the basin of the East Fork of the Crystal River. The backpacking route around the

Maroon Bells follows the trail into this basin. It then climbs to cross Frigid Air Pass. It continues over Trail Rider Pass and Buckskin Pass on the return to the Maroon Lake parking area.

However, since we're allowing only one day for this hike, return the way you came.

Crater Lake and the West Maroon Creek valley, on the way to West Maroon Pass.

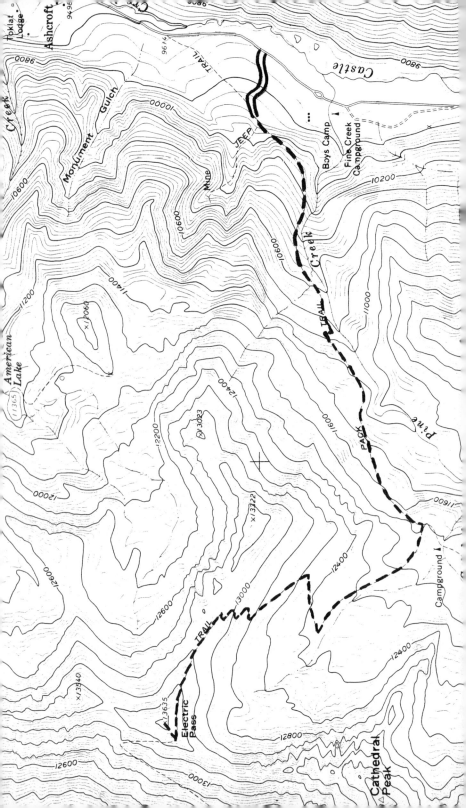

49. ELECTRIC PASS AND ELECTRIC PASS PEAK

Distance: 11 miles (out and back)
Starting elevation: 9,880 feet
High point: 13,635 feet
Elevation gain: 3,800 feet
Rating: moderate, easy trail walking, but steep in spots
  and with large elevation gain
Time allowed: 8 or 9 hours
Maps: 7.5 minute Hayden Peak
     White River National Forest

This long trek has been described as being on the dull side, just a long grind up a trail. However, it's much more interesting than that and is included here for several reasons. First, it gives you an opportunity to reach what is believed to be the highest named pass in the state. It also brings you to the highest summit in the Elk Range that can be reached almost all on trail. Finally, the views, both along the way and from the top are spectacular.

Electric Pass is said to be named by a Forest Service ranger after escaping from electric shock during a storm. You can experience static electricity because of the high mineral content of the rocks. Static electricity can make you hair stand on end and cause buzzing sounds on any metal in your clothing. Static electricity means that a storm is in the vicinity, so it's best to go back down right away.

The trail for this hike goes up through an aspen and pine forest, then climbs steeply along the rushing waters of Pine Creek. There are good views of Cathedral Lake and impressive cliffs in the background as the trail climbs into a vast basin and Electric Pass comes into view. The trail continues up this basin as it climbs the flanks of Electric Pass Peak, an unimposing, rounded summit in contrast to the many more rugged peaks of the Elk Range.

The trailhead is off the Ashcroft road south of Aspen. From a half mile west of the Castle Creek bridge in Aspen on Colorado 82, turn south on the paved road, then make an immediate left turn toward Ashcroft. Continue on pavement for twelve miles. A mile beyond Ashcroft, turn right, through a gate, onto an unpaved road. This

View from Electric Pass Peak, with Electric Pass in the foreground, Cathedral Peak down the ridge, and Castle Peak in the distance.

road can be driven a bit over a half mile to a parking area at the trailhead.

From this trailhead, trails lead to two destinations—Cathedral Lake and Electric Pass. The topographic map would indicate that there is only one point of decision on the five-mile trail to Electric Pass. About halfway, at 11,800 feet, a left fork goes southwest to Cathedral Lake, while the Electric Pass Trail heads to the right and bears northwest. However, there are a number of trails in the Cathedral Lake area that are not shown on the map. Taking the right-hand fork each time in this area will lead you toward Electric Pass.

The Electric Pass Trail climbs over the ridge between 13,943-foot Cathedral Peak to the south and the 13,635-foot summit known unofficially as Electric Pass Peak to the north. The low point on this ridge is 13,300 feet. However, because of the steep cliffs in the vicinity of the low point, the trail climbs high on the south flank of Electric Pass Peak and crosses the ridge at 13,500 feet. From the

On the trail along Castle Creek, near the beginning of the hike to Electric Pass.

pass, it's only 135 feet of climbing up the easy ridge to get to the summit of Electric Pass Peak.

As you approach the pass, you get a good view of Cathedral Peak on the left and the ragged, pinnacled ridges extending from it. When you reach the pass, a spectacular view of the western part of the Elk Range unfolds, with the Fourteeners North and South Maroon, Pyramid, Snowmass, and Capitol standing out. You can look down into the Conundrum Creek valley, which has a long trail leading to Conundrum Hot Springs. The trail down from Electric Pass meets the Conundrum Creek Trail. From Electric Pass Peak, there is a smooth ridge leading north to Hayden Peak. After absorbing all of these views, it's back to the trail for the return by the way you came.

If you are making this hike when there is a large, steep snowfield over the trail just before the pass, it's best to leave the trail and go up the east ridge directly to Electric Pass Peak. You can safely come down the ridge to the pass, west of the snowfield.

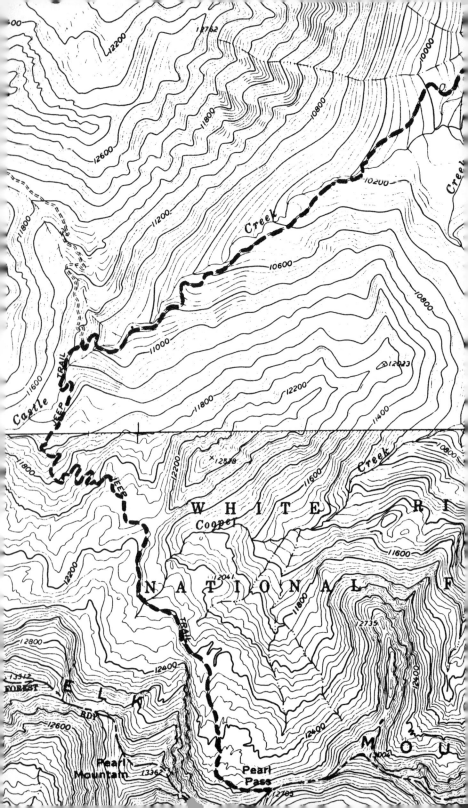

50. PEARL PASS

Distance: 11 miles (out and back)
Starting elevation: 9,780 feet
High point: 12,705 feet
Elevation gain: 2,950 feet
Rating: easy
Time allowed: 8 hours
Maps: 7.5 minute Hayden Peak
7.5 minute Pearl Pass
White River National Forest

This hike is the only one in this book that is entirely on 4WD road. However, the road is passable all the way by 4WD vehicles for only a small portion of the summer and not at all in some years. This historic old wagon road is an interesting route through a scenic cirque on the north side of the ridge separating the Aspen and Crested Butte areas. It makes a better hike than a 4WD trip. The starting point is off the Ashcroft road south of Aspen. Proceed a half mile west of the Castle Creek bridge in Aspen on Colorado 82, then turn south and make an immediate left turn toward Ashcroft, leaving the Maroon Lake road. Follow the road through Ashcroft for a total of thirteen miles to a junction bearing to the right. After the junction, the gravel road soon deteriorates so that regular cars should be parked within the first mile.

Walk up this road, which follows Castle Creek. At about a mile, there's a ford of Castle Creek, with a foot bridge for hikers. The ford is the end of the line for cars and may be difficult for 4WDs. Another mile and a half on gentle grades brings you to a junction. The right fork leads to Montezuma Mine and is the route usually followed for a climb of Castle Peak, the highest peak in the Elk Range.

The route to Pearl Pass follows the left fork. The road steepens as it climbs from the junction at 11,150 feet to reach a grassy saddle at 12,140 feet. You may think that you're approaching Pearl Pass as you climb to this point, but there's still a ways to go.

The rest of the route is obvious. From the 12,140-foot saddle, you can see the old road curve around the right side of the cliffs in the scenic cirque to Pearl Pass. It's in this section that the snow-

Road up Castle Creek to the Pearl Pass trailhead.

banks remain until late summer, effectively blocking travel by vehicles. In fact, an early season trip to Pearl Pass will require some sidehill traverses over the snow.

From Pearl Pass, the route descends southward into the Middle Brush Creek valley and leads on to the Crested Butte area. Admire the scenic view of the green valley of Middle Brush Creek, rest a bit, and return across the barren, rocky cirque and on down the way you came.

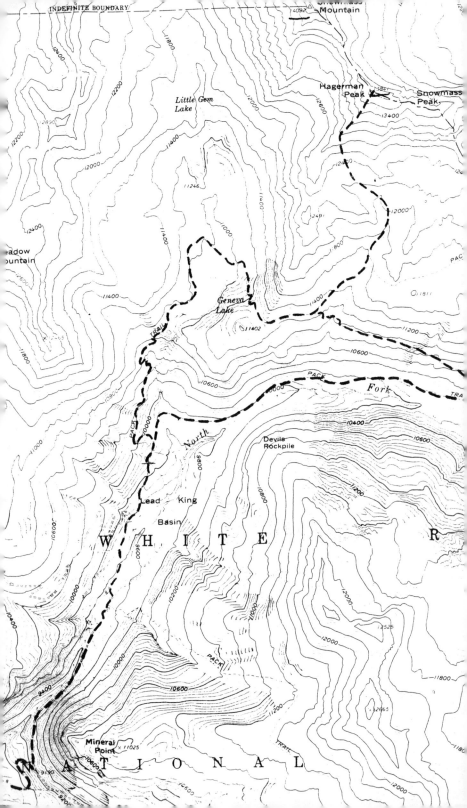

51. GENEVA LAKE AND HAGERMAN PEAK

Distance: 15 miles (dumbbell loop)
Starting elevation: 9,000 feet
High point: 13,841 feet
Elevation gain: 5,000 feet
Rating: difficult, because of length and large elevation gain
Time allowed: 12 to 14 hours
Maps: 7.5 minute Snowmass Mountain
White River National Forest

This long, strenuous trek to a high peak in the western part of the Elk Range gives a varied experience. First is a drive to two interesting small towns. Next is a walk or drive over a rugged 4WD road, followed by a hike up an interesting trail to a beautiful lake. Then a trail through the forest leads to a ridge ascent of one of the highest hundred peaks in the state. Another trail provides a different route for the return.

Drive Colorado 133 for twenty-two miles south of Carbondale, or forty-four miles north of Hotchkiss, which is at the intersection with Colorado 92. Turn east for six miles on a paved road to the town of Marble, and continue for five and a half miles on unpaved road to the small settlement of Crystal. The last part of this tour is sometimes rough, but two-wheel-drive cars regularly make it. Be sure to take a right fork at two miles beyond Marble to follow along the Crystal River. The stopping point for most vehicles is about one-fourth mile beyond Crystal at a large flat area on the right. Park here.

Walk up the 4WD road, making a sharp left turn toward the north within a quarter of a mile, where the road to the southeast leads to Schofield Pass. At one mile, take the left fork over a bridge. Continue less than a half mile to where the road makes a sharp switchback to the south at a parking area at 9,700 feet in Lead King Basin. With 4WD and determination to drive the rough road, your hike can start from here, saving three miles of walking on the round trip and 700 feet of elevation gain.

Follow one of several trails northward, taking a left fork at a half

Snowmass Mountain from the summit of Hagerman Peak.

mile, after the various trails have joined into a single one. Climb the hill on switchbacks with excellent views of several waterfalls below Geneva Lake. Continue on the trail to circle the scenic lake on the west, pass its many good campsites, cross the north inlet of the lake, and head east to reenter the forest. From the area north of the lake, there are good views of 14,092-foot Snowmass Mountain to the north, with Hagerman Peak to the right.

After breaking out into the open beyond the section through the forest, take a left fork following a level stretch at 11,300 feet. Continue on the trail less than a half mile until it crosses a drainage from the north at 11,480 feet. Leave the trail and follow this drainage northward. Continue for a half mile, rounding the nose of a minor ridge extending from the west. At about 12,000 feet, bear to the left to gain the broad south ridge of Hagerman Peak. Continue up this ridge as it bears north and slightly eastward to the summit.

From the summit, there's a good view of Snowmass Lake to the east. Snowmass Mountain is along the ridge to the northwest. The

Snowmass Mountain, with its large snowfield, and Hagerman Peak to the left, as seen from the ridge north of Buckskin Pass. (photo by Bill Bueler)

normal route for climbing Snowmass Mountain involves a backpack to Snowmass Lake. From Snowmass Lake, the predominant view is of Hagerman Peak, but Hagerman Peak is much less frequently climbed than the higher Snowmass Mountain.

After returning to the trail, you can use an interesting alternate return route. It's a bit longer and not quite so scenic, but it takes you into another valley. At the trail junction at 11,300 feet, just below the point where you left the trail, take the left fork toward the east. This leads down into the valley of the North Fork of the Crystal River, meeting the trail into Fravert Basin. At the junction with this trail, at 10,350 feet, make a right turn to follow the North Fork Trail back to the junction a half mile north of the 4WD road in Lead King Basin.

This long hike is easier in the latter part of the summer, after the snowbanks have melted from the trail. The ascent of Hagerman Peak is better after the main snowmelt, when the ascent route is dry. If this entire hike is too strenuous, the loop trip without the ascent of Hagerman Peak makes an excellent hike.

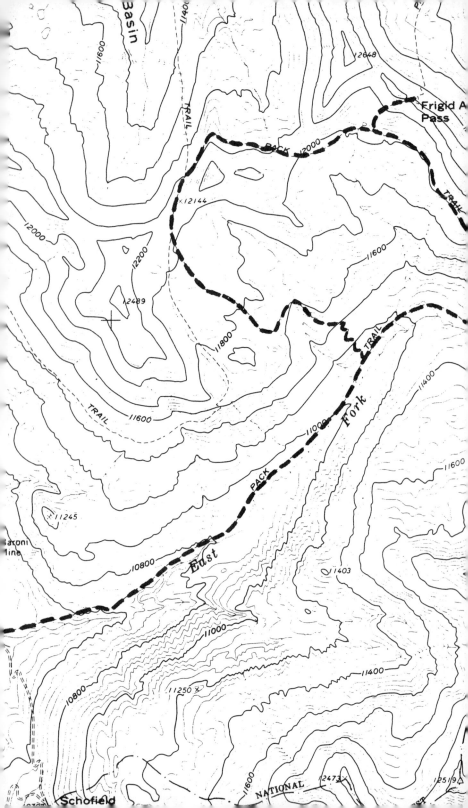

52. FRIGID AIR PASS

Distance: 8 miles (dumbbell loop)
Starting elevation: 10,400 feet
High point: 12,380 feet
Elevation gain: 2,400 feet
Rating: easy
Time allowed: 6 hours
Maps: 7.5 minute Snowmass Mountain
White River National Forest

You're on trail all the way for this hike. First, you visit a scenic pass west of the Maroon Bells. Then there's an interesting route along a ridge to an unnamed pass, from which you return to the valley to complete a loop. As a bonus, to get to the trailhead, you have a scenic auto trip over another interesting pass.

The trailhead is at Schofield Park. From Crested Butte, go north eight miles to Gothic, and continue another six miles to Schofield Pass, which is at 10,707 feet. Another mile to the north, down from Schofield Pass, brings you to the edge of Schofield Park, a vast flat area. The road from Gothic to Schofield Pass, and particularly the mile beyond, may not be suitable for passenger cars at all times. You may want to check locally.

As you enter Schofield Park, look for a road leading to the right just beyond a creek crossing. This road provides some good parking places within the first hundred yards.

While 4WD vehicles can go a bit further, it's best to walk up this road to the east. The road soon turns to trail as the route follows the north side of the East Fork of the Crystal River. There are several trails through this section, and it really doesn't matter which one you follow, as they eventually join into a single trail.

About two miles from the trailhead, after climbing to 11,100 feet, you'll reach a junction. Continue straight ahead on the right fork, as the other fork leads up the hill to the left. The left trail going uphill is the one we'll be returning on for this loop trip.

Another three-quarters of a mile leads to a "T," with the trail contouring along the hillside both to the right and the left. The route to the right goes to West Maroon Pass, which is approached from the other side in hike number 48. The route to Frigid Air Pass is to the left.

Maroon Bells from Frigid Air Pass. (photo by Bill Bueler)

For the next mile, the trail contours along the south side of the ridge, gaining altitude slowly. Then there's another trail junction, from which the route takes the right fork to climb steeply to Frigid Air Pass. This pass is aptly named, if you happen to be there when a cool wind flows over the pass.

From Frigid Air Pass, the valley to the north is Fravert Basin. You can get a close-up view of the Maroon Bells, only two miles away to the northeast. This view of the southwest side of the Maroon Bells is interestingly different from the much-photographed one from Maroon Lake on the northeast side.

You could return by the same route, but an interesting loop trip provides some variation. Return south down the steep trail from the pass to the first trail junction. Turn right to go south of a small lakelet, and follow this trail westward to an unnamed pass at 12,060 feet. Then continue on a trail to the north side of two ridge points, circling to still another pass at 12,100 feet.

Just before you reach this 12,100 foot pass, you'll join a trail coming up from the valley to the north. The trail that you join comes out of Hasley Basin. Continue south. The pass that the trail crosses is sometimes referred to a Hasley Pass. Across Hasley Basin to the north is Hagerman Peak, and beyond it is the slightly higher Snowmass Mountain.

From Hasley Pass, the route back is to the southeast. There's another trail junction just after you leave the pass, where you take the left fork. Following this trail, you then descend to reach the trail junction at 11,100 feet. You then go back to the southwest along the East Fork of the Crystal River, following the route that you came on from Schofield Park.

53. COPPER PASS AND TRIANGLE PASS

Distance: 17 miles (out and back)
Starting elevation: 9,820 feet
High point: 12,900 feet
Elevation gain: 3,500 feet
Rating: moderate, long, but all on trail
Time allowed: 10 hours
Maps: 7.5 minute Gothic
7.5 minute Maroon Bells
Gunnison National Forest

This is a long hike, but it's entirely on good trail. It provides outstanding views as it takes you deep into remote country.

Drive to Gothic, eight miles north of Crested Butte. Continue another half mile north of Gothic to a side road on the right. Drive past a parking area at the start of this road and proceed a half mile on the narrow rough winding road as it climbs to a trailhead parking area.

Hike generally eastward along the up and down trail. This trail, built in recent years, will lead you in a mile to join an old road from Gothic to Judd Falls. There's a stone bench to rest on and view the falls, but if you need much of a rest already, then this hike is too long for you.

The closed 4WD road in the Maroon Bells—Snowmass Wilderness is the route for the next several miles as it climbs along Copper Creek. You stay in the timber until almost 11,500 feet. In this area there are several routes bearing to the left. One dead-end road leads to mines and lakelets on the side of Avery Peak. Farther up, the old road continues straight ahead up the hill toward Copper Lake and East Maroon Pass, but our route bears to the right. It continues through the forest to finally emerge where another trail goes to the left.

The trail becomes more rocky as it circles the basin to the north of White Rock Mountain. It climbs along this basin in a long straight stretch before turning to the north. Shortly after the turn to the north, look for a spur trail turning sharply to the left. Follow this spur trail to reach Copper Pass in less than a hundred yards. From Copper Pass at 12,580 feet, the view is into the East Maroon Creek Basin.

Looking into the East Maroon Creek valley from Copper Pass. The Maroon Bells are on the left and Pyramid Peak is the high point on the right.

From Copper Pass, return to the route to Triangle Pass. Continue around the basin for a little over a half mile to reach Triangle Pass. This pass, sometimes called Conundrum Pass, provides a view into the Conundrum Creek valley. About two miles down the trail into the valley is Conundrum Hot Springs. The hot springs make an attractive destination for backpackers, so there may be more foot traffic than you'd expect on a trail of this length. The approach to the hot springs up the Conundrum Creek valley from the north is about as long as this route from Gothic.

The trail through the stark cirque from Copper Pass to Triangle Pass.

From Triangle Pass, there's yet another pass that you can see—Coffeepot Pass, 12,740 feet—down the ridge to the southeast. Coffeepot Pass is between the Conundrum Creek valley and the West Brush Creek valley to the south, which is in the Taylor River country.

For this hike, return the way you came, as there's really no alternate route unless you want to make a long backpack into the valleys to the north.

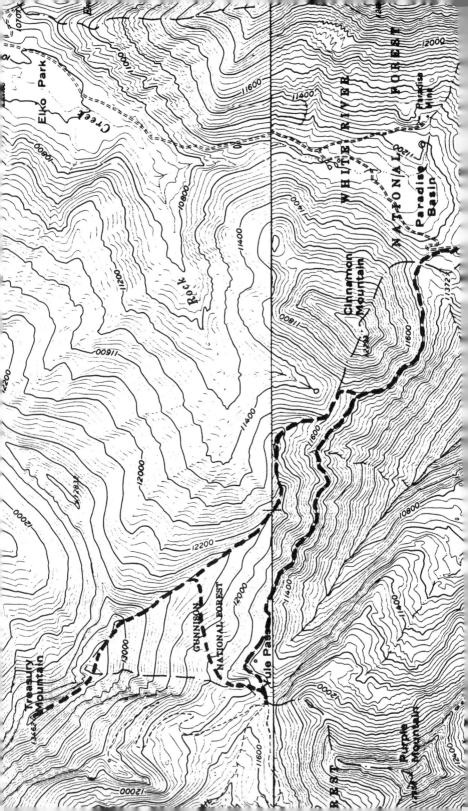

54. YULE PASS AND TREASURY MOUNTAIN

Distance: 6 miles (loop)
Starting elevation: 11,260 feet
High point: 13,462 feet
Elevation gain: 2,300 feet
Rating: moderate
Time allowed: 7 hours
Maps: 7.5 minute Oh-be-Joyful
      7.5 minute Snowmass Mountain
      White River National Forest
      Gunnison National Forest

This hike combines an easy two-mile walk to a scenic pass, a stiff hillside climb to a high-mountain flat area, and an interesting ridge walk to a high summit. The descent follows a different route down a broad ridge.

The trailhead is at Paradise Divide, 11,260 feet, a scenic pass that is unnamed on the maps. Paradise Divide is two and one-half miles south of Schofield Pass.

The route for regular cars to 10,707-foot Schofield Pass is from Crested Butte. Follow the road northeast through the ski area for eight miles to Gothic and six more miles to Schofield Pass. Schofield Pass can also be reached by 4WD from the west through Marble and Crystal. However, the route between Crystal and the pass, the scene of one of the worst 4WD accidents in Colorado history, is definitely not recommended.

The route from Schofield Pass to Paradise Divide usually can be negotiated by smaller cars after the snows are gone. Go down the west side from Schofield Pass less than a quarter of a mile to take the left fork at a junction. After about a mile, take the left fork at another junction. The road to the right, not shown on the topographic map, goes up Rock Creek.

Cross Rock Creek to the east, and ascend on the west side of a hill. Paradise Divide, a recognizable pass between two high points, is reached after another mile and a half. Park here.

Paradise Divide can also be reached by a road, Gunnison County 734, coming in from the south. This road turns west from

Looking northeast from Treasury Mountain. (photo by Bill Bueler)

the Crested Butte-Gothic road about a mile beyond Crested Butte. Currently, this approach is over a better quality road.

Just north of the small lake at Paradise Divide, find a 4WD road leading north and turning sharply west. Hike along this road, which contours along the south side of Cinnamon Mountain. While this road could be driven a quarter mile or so, you'll soon come to the first of several rockslides that currently limit the road to foot traffic.

In the two miles to Yule Pass, the route overlooks the scenic Slate River valley. It gives a good view of 12,958-foot Purple Mountain, aptly named, which stands to the left of Yule Pass.

When 11,700-foot Yule Pass is reached, there's a fine view of the Yule Creek valley, with three distinct trails. The left and right ones go to mine properties, while the middle one starts down toward Marble, eight miles away. To continue toward Treasury Mountain, go back about an eighth of a mile to find gentle climbing up the slopes to the north. From here, there is no trail, and the grade is sometimes steep. The best route is to bear somewhat to the right of the south ridge. The next goal is to reach the crest of the ridge leading in from the southeast. Upon reaching this ridge at about 12,500 feet, turn left, or northwest, to continue to a broad flat area southeast of Treasury Mountain. Cross this area northwest to the obvious ridge, which may be followed to the summit. This ridge provides good walking if you carefully select the route.

From the summit, you can see the ridge leading northwest to a 13,407-foot ridge point and from there on to the broad and slightly higher Treasure Mountain at 13,528 feet. Good views of the Maroon Bells and Snowmass Mountain are to the northeast and north.

For the return, a somewhat different route is suggested. After crossing the flat area below the summit ridge, continue on down the ridge to the southeast. This broad ridge offers good walking with only a few slow sections. When you reach a low point between Treasury Mountain and Cinnamon Mountain ahead, you'll find a drainage that provides a good descent to the right, leading back to the road between Paradise Divide and Yule Pass. A turn to the left and a three-quarter mile walk bring you back to the trailhead.

If you are unable to drive beyond Schofield Pass, this is still a satisfactory all-day hike. With the added walk to and from Paradise Divide, the round-trip distance is about eleven miles, and the elevation gain is 2,800 feet.

We would recommend the southern approach if you want to have a better chance of driving all the way to Paradise Divide. By following the southern route, however, you miss the scenic trip over historic Schofield Pass.

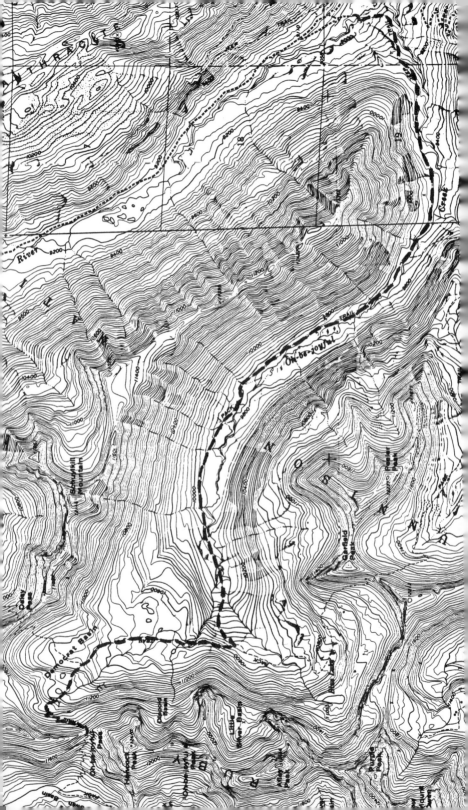

55. OH-BE-JOYFUL PASS

Distance: 14 miles (out and back)
Starting elevation: 8,940 feet
High point: 11,740 feet
Elevation gain: 3,000 feet
Rating: moderate, because of distance and elevation
  gain
Time allowed: 8 or 9 hours
Maps: 7.5 minute Oh-be-joyful
       Gunnison National Forest

We wanted to end this book on a happy note, so we've chosen Oh-be-joyful Pass as the last hike. It may not be the most scenic pass in Colorado, but it certainly has the most picturesque name. Part of the hike follows a sometimes-driveable 4WD route up Oh-be-joyful Creek into a very beautiful valley. While there is a good bit of altitude to be gained, it's spread over quite a few miles, so the grade isn't too steep. A potential problem is the initial water crossing during the early season runoff. Thus, this is a better late summer or early fall hike.

The trailhead is near Crested Butte. Drive north from town toward the ski area on the road to Gothic, and turn left after almost a mile. Follow this road, Gunnison County 734, along the Slate River for four and a half miles to a junction on the left. This road turns back sharply to the south and leads down the hill to a small camping area on the east side of Slate River.

At this point, the 4WD road fords the Slate River and leads along the north side of Oh-be-joyful Creek. If the water is too high to safely cross, this is not a good starting point for the hike. Another possibility is to backtrack along the Slate River road for a mile to the Gunsight Pass road. This road leaves the Slate River road at a sharp angle to the north and, after a switchback, crosses the Slate River on a bridge. After this crossing, continue on this road to the end of the next switchback in the vicinity of some old mine buildings and abandoned equipment.

At this point you are near the 4WD road, but it is to the north across Oh-be-joyful Creek. So head northwest through the timber to reach the creek. Continue west along the creek to find a suitable crossing. If the water in both Slate River and Oh-be-joyful Creek is very high, the best crossing of Oh-be-joyful Creek is near the point it empties into Slate River. In this area the creek widens out, so that a safe crossing by wading can be made. This crossing is reached by leaving the Gunsight Pass road between the Slate River bridge and the mine buildings, to follow a trail northwest along the southwest side of Oh-be-joyful Creek. Once across the creek, it's an easy walk uphill to meet the 4WD road. Continue west along this road.

If you've succeeded in crossing Slate River or Oh-be-joyful Creek at a time when 4WD vehicles can't cross the Slate River, you may be all alone during the rest of this beautiful hike.

After one and a quarter miles from the Slate River crossing, the 4WD road reaches a parking area. Only the most hardy 4WD vehicle drivers continue beyond this point, and then only during optimum conditions. Beyond the parking area, the 4WD road goes through a succession of bogs, narrow passages through the forest, and steep slopes. Past cattle grazing has created a multitude of trails bypassing these difficult sections of 4WD road, making hiking more pleasant than driving.

As the route continues west, northwest, and then west again along Oh-be-joyful Creek, a succession of waterfalls can be seen. Pyramid-shaped Peeler Peak stands out to the left. As the route along the 4WD road swings back to the west, you reach an open area giving good views of Democrat Basin ahead.

After crossing several side creeks that enter Oh-be-joyful Creek from the right, a cabin in a clearing is reached. Soon the old road begins to climb more steeply through the forest, and then becomes only a trail as the route reaches a trail junction at 10,500 feet. The trail to the left goes over a pass south of Garfield Peak. From a few steps left of the junction the switchbacks leading out of the impressive basin to the south can be seen.

Our route is to the right, heading north into Democrat Basin. Soon the extent of this scenic basin becomes apparent. The trail climbs over rock outcrops, crosses small streams and passes numerous small lakes. Straight ahead the switchback trail climbing the grassy slopes to Daisy Pass can be seen.

High in Democrat Basin, the trail junction of the Daisy Pass and Oh-be-joyful Pass is reached, but this point may be difficult to locate. In any event, the Daisy Pass Trail continues to the north, while our trail to Oh-be-joyful Pass heads left, or to the west.

After climbing a small bench and passing by two small lakes, the trail takes a long switchback to the south before the final short, steep, gravel climb to Oh-be-joyful Pass.

The view to the west from the broad pass is impressive. Marcellina Mountain stands out as the centerpiece. The broad valleys on either side are particularly colorful as the aspen are turning color.

The trail continues down the west side from the pass into Swan Basin. After viewing the sights, return the way you came.

APPENDIX
Additional Hikes in Central Colorado

In the introduction, we said that we had difficulty in choosing the fifty-five hikes described in this book from the hundreds of hikes Dotty and I have taken in central Colorado. Several people have suggested that we describe some of the other hikes, particularly trail hikes.

Here is a sampling of the many other fine hikes in the central Colorado area. These trail hikes provide fine hiking even if you go only part way and do not reach the indicated destination. Road and trail numbers are from National Forest maps.

1. Rich Creek loop—From near Weston Pass Campground on road 425 between US 285 and Weston Pass, hike up Rich Creek on trail 616 and back on Rough and Tumbling Creek trail 617.

2. Mystic Island Lake—From Fulford Cave Campground south of Eagle, hike southwest on trail 1899 to the lake.

3. Mt. Thomas trail—From near Crooked Creek Pass south of Eagle, hike west on trail 1870.

4. Eagle Lake—From southwest of Woods Lake on road 507 southeast of Crooked Creek Pass, hike northeast and east on trail 1915 to the lake.

5. Cross Creek—From road 707 between US 24 and Half Moon Campground, hike the long trail 2006 south along Cross Creek.

6. Half Moon Pass—From Half Moon Campground south of Mintern, hike south and west on the trail 2009 to the pass.

7. Lake Constantine—From Half Moon Campground, hike south on trail 2001 to the lake.

8. Timberline Lake—West of Leadville on the road curve west of Turquoise Lake, hike the trail (old road 146) west and north to Timberline Lake.

9. Fryingpan Lakes—From the end of road 505 southeast of Thomasville, hike southeast and south to the lakes.

10. Mt. Massive trail—From near Elbert Creek Campground southwest of Leadville, hike north on the Colorado Trail and west on trail 1379 toward Mount Massive.

11. Mt. Elbert trail—From near Elbert Creek Campground, hike south on the Colorado Trail and either continue south or take a right fork toward Mount Elbert.

12. Black Cloud Creek—From Colorado 82 west of Twin Lakes, hike trail 1439 up Black Cloud Creek toward Bull Hill.

13. Kroenke Lake—Drive west on the North Cottonwood Creek road as in hike number 27 and continue to road's end. Hike west, taking the left fork at a trail junction and continue to Kroenke Lake.

14. Bear Lake—Proceed as in the hike to Kroenke Lake, but take the right fork at the trail junction and hike to Bear Lake on the route to Mount Harvard.

15. Timberline Trail—Drive to the trailhead between Taylor Park Reservoir and Cottonwood Pass and hike south or north on the Timberline Trail.

16. Rosebud Gulch—From road 744 west of Taylor Park Reservoir, hike west on road 744-21 and trail 423.

17. Hughes Creek—From the Avalanche Trailhead on Chaffee County road 306 west of Buena Vista, hike the Colorado Trail north to a high pass to meet a route up Mount Yale (see hike number 29).

18. Browns Creek trail—From US 285 south of Nathrop, follow forest roads 252 and 255 (Chaffee County roads 270 and 272) to the trailhead and hike trail 1385 westward.

19. Poplar Gulch—From St. Elmo, hike trail 1368 north to a saddle, where the trail continues down Green Timber Gulch (see hike number 35).

20. Angel of Shavano Campground area—From road 214 along North Fork South Arkansas River, hike north from near the campground on trail 1776.

21. Boulder Lake—From Gold Creek Campground (see hike number 43), follow the Fossil Ridge trail west and take a spur trail north to the lake.

22. Horsethief Lake—From road 748 northwest of Taylor Park Reservoir, hike trail 411 to the lake.

23. Waterdog Lakes—From US 50 between Monarch Pass and Monarch, hike west on trail 1365 to the lakes.

24. South Fooses Creek—From US 50 between Maysville and Garfield, drive southwest on road 238 to a trailhead and hike trail 1362, a portion of the Colorado Trail, to the Continental Divide.

25. Green Creek—From US 50 west of Poncha Springs, drive southwest on road 239 and hike trail 1361 to the Continental Divide.

26. Little Cochetopa Creek—From US 50 west of Poncha Springs, drive south on road 241. Trail 1359 that leads to the Continental Divide begins at the end of this rough road.

27. East Snowmass Creek—From a trailhead along Snowmass Creek south of the town of Snowmass, hike south on long trail 1977.

28. East Maroon Creek—From the Maroon Creek road, hike the long trail 1983 south to East Maroon Pass.

29. American Lake—From the Castle Creek road south of Aspen, hike the trail southwest to the lake.

Index